CU00642536

"This scientifically-grounded behavioural coaching practice! Written by two leading wonderfully accessible book that will introd powerful, process-based approach to coachi features and providing a comprehensive roa Whether you're coaching individuals or g towards personal improvement, this incred your coaching sessions; adding another powe ...., .. your coachees' tool boxes. All coaches should grab a copy without delay. Highly recommended."

Dr Michael Sinclair, Director of City Psychology Group; author of
Mindfulness for Busy People* and *The Little ACT Workbook

"How do we coach people to work practically toward their chosen life directions, while skillfully responding to the emotions and thoughts that arise from these choices? Coaches who are looking for evidence-based ways to work will find this book an essential guide.

The authors provide a very clear introduction to Acceptance and Commitment Coaching, outlining a model of practice, and a philosophy toward coaching that is pragmatic and flexible (contextual behavioural science). They also provide an accessible and entertaining introduction to learning principles based on Relational Frame Theory. This description of how language works in practice will help coaches to do their job using powerful and precise change methods.

The book contains various enlightening and useful examples given of how to engage learners in the six core processes of Acceptance and Commitment Coaching. The authors also provide pointers on mistakes they have made in coaching, sharing their experience and wisdom, and helping the reader to gain a deeper understanding of this unique coaching model. The principles described here will lead to transformative changes for learner and coach alike."

Eric Morris, PhD, Director, La Trobe University Psychology
Clinic, Melbourne, Australia

"Having recommended the authors' previous book, *ACTivate Your Life,* to many of my therapy clients, it was no surprise to see that this book is full of the same clear descriptions of ACT and its application, this time to using it as an approach to coaching. This will be a valuable resource to coaches out there looking to introduce a coherent model of human function into their practice."

Dr Richard Bennett, Chartered Psychologist, British Psychological Society, UK

"This is an excellent book for anyone who wants to use the ACT model for coaching. Easy-to-read, highly practical, loaded with simple but powerful tools and techniques. If you're already a coach, this will surely supercharge the way you work. And if you want to start coaching but aren't sure how, this book will show you the way."

Russ Harris, author of *ACT Made Simple* and *The Happiness Trap*

"This book is interesting, well-written, thorough and timely. In fact, I am confident that any coach who reads it will immediately be able to incorporate, and see the benefits of, the ACC model with their coaches."

Dr Nic Hooper, Senior Lecturer at the University of the West of England, UK;
co-author of *The Research Journey of Acceptance and Commitment Therapy*

Acceptance and Commitment Coaching

Jon Hill and Joe Oliver introduce the Acceptance and Commitment Coaching (ACC) model with clarity and accessibility, defining it as an approach that incorporates mindfulness and acceptance, focusing on committed, values-based actions to help coachees make meaningful changes to their lives.

Acceptance and Commitment Coaching: Distinctive Features explains the ACC model in such a way that the reader will be able to put it into practice immediately, as well as offering sufficient context to anchor the practical tools in a clear theoretical framework. Split into two parts, the book begins by emphasising ACC's relevance and its core philosophy before providing an overview of its key theoretical points and the research that supports it. The authors also explain the six key ACC processes: defusion, acceptance, contact with the present moment, self as context, values and committed action, and explain how to use them in practice. Hill and Oliver address essential topics, such as the critical work needed before and as you begin working with a coachee, how to use metaphor as an effective tool as a coach, and they finish by offering helpful tips on how to help coachees maintain their positive changes, how to make ACC accessible to all types of client, how to manage challenging coachees and how to work with both individuals and groups using ACC. Aimed specifically at coaches, the book offers context, examples, practicality and a unique combination of practical and theoretical points in a concise format.

Acceptance and Commitment Coaching: Distinctive Features is essential reading for coaches, coaching psychologists and executive coaches in practice and in training. It would be of interest to academics and students of coaching psychology and coaching techniques, as well as Acceptance and Commitment Therapy (ACT) practitioners looking to move into coaching.

Jon Hill is a corporate trainer and executive coach, and the founder of Blueprint Coaching and Training Ltd, working with companies around the world to improve resilience, well-being and psychological flexibility.

Dr Joe Oliver is a Consultant Clinical Psychologist and founder of Contextual Consulting, the leading provider of ACT training in the United Kingdom. He has worked for over 20 years as a practising psychologist and is currently a course director at University College London. He also runs a busy London-based private practice, offering ACT coaching and consultations.

Coaching Distinctive Features
Series Editor: Windy Dryden

Leading practitioners and theorists of coaching approaches write simply and briefly on what constitutes the main features of their particular approach. Each book highlights 30 main features, divided between theoretical and practical points. Written in a straightforward and accessible style, they can be understood by both those steeped in the coaching tradition and by those outside that tradition. The series editor is Windy Dryden.

Titles in the series:

Rational Emotive Behavioural Coaching by Windy Dryden

Cognitive Behavioural Coaching by Michael Neenan

Acceptance and Commitment Coaching by Jon Hill and Joe Oliver

For further information about this series please visit
www.routledge.com/Coaching-Distinctive-Features/book-series/CDF

Acceptance and Commitment Coaching

Distinctive Features

Jon Hill and Joe Oliver

Routledge
Taylor & Francis Group

LONDON AND NEW YORK

First published 2019
by Routledge
2 Park Square, Milton Park, Abingdon, Oxon OX14 4RN

and by Routledge
52 Vanderbilt Avenue, New York, NY 10017

Routledge is an imprint of the Taylor & Francis Group, an informa business

British Library Cataloguing-in-Publication Data
A catalogue record for this book is available from the British Library

Library of Congress Cataloging-in-Publication Data
Names: Hill, Jon, 1977- author. | Oliver, Joe, 1975- author.
Title: Acceptance and commitment coaching : distinctive features / Jon Hill and Joe Oliver.
Description: Abingdon, Oxon ; New York, NY : Routledge, [2019] | Includes bibliographical references and index. | Description based on print version record and CIP data provided by publisher; resource not viewed.
Identifiers: LCCN 2018039386 (print) | LCCN 2018053790 (ebook) |
ISBN 9781315122724 (Master ebook) | ISBN 9781351346177 (Adobe Reader) |
ISBN 9781351346160 (ePub) | ISBN 9781351346153 (Mobipocket) |
ISBN 9781138564978 | ISBN 9781138564978(hardback) |
ISBN 9781138564985(pbk.) | ISBN 9781315122724(ebook)
Subjects: LCSH: Personal coaching. | Motivation (Psychology) |
Acceptance and commitment therapy.
Classification: LCC BF637.P36 (ebook) | LCC BF637.P36 H56 2019 (print) |
DDC 158.3–dc23
LC record available at https://lccn.loc.gov/2018039386

ISBN: 978-1-138-56497-8 (hbk)
ISBN: 978-1-138-56498-5 (pbk)
ISBN: 978-1-315-12272-4 (ebk)

Typeset in Times New Roman
by Swales & Willis Ltd

Contents

Introduction

Acceptance and Commitment Coaching (ACC) is a model of coaching based on the principles of Acceptance and Commitment Therapy (ACT). ACT is a psychotherapeutic approach that uses mindfulness and acceptance, and a focus on committed, values-based action to help people to make changes in their lives.

ACT has become a widely used model in clinical settings, largely because of the extensive body of research demonstrating its effectiveness across an incredibly broad range of issues, including psychosis, depression, anxiety, substance misuse and addiction, anger and chronic pain. It is this evidence-base and essential versatility that makes ACT so well suited to coaching, and which has led to a growing number of coaches adopting ACC as their primary way of working with individual and private coachees in the workplace, in the world of sport and beyond. There is now a burgeoning body of evidence demonstrating the effectiveness of ACT-related interventions in areas such as workplace well-being, resilience and performance.

In this book we will describe the core ACC philosophy and make a case for its relevance and value to the world of coaching (Chapters 1 and 2), before offering an overview of the key theoretical underpinnings of the model and the research supporting it (Chapters 3 to 5). We will also explain the principles of the six key ACC processes of defusion, acceptance, contact with the present moment, self as context, values and committed action (Chapters 6 to 11). We will then move into addressing the vital work to be done with coachees before and as you begin coaching (Chapters 12 to 16), before describing one of the most important tools available to the ACC coach – the metaphor (Chapter 17). We then expand on how to practically implement the six core ACC processes (Chapters 18 to 23), and offer some tips on how to help coachees maintain changes (Chapter 24). Finally, we offer some practical advice for how to make ACC accessible to busy or high-performing coachees (Chapters 25 and 26), how to manage or avoid the challenging moments that can show up when working with ACC (Chapters 27 and 28) and tips on coaching with individuals and groups (Chapters 29 and 30).

Our intention is that this book will be a helpful resource to coaches who wish to adopt the ACC model in its entirety, or who would simply like to incorporate aspects of it into their current way of working. As we will go on to describe, one of the key strengths of ACC is that it is based on a coherent model of change, so consciously adopting and following the model as it is described here will likely be the most reliable way of helping your coachees get the results they want. *And* the model also offers versatility, flexibility and a range of different ways to help coachees get unstuck and make real positive changes in their lives. Our main hope is that this book can be a means to help you be more effective, creative and conscious in the way that you coach.

Acknowledgements

Any endeavour such as this is truly cooperative and requires the time, energy and input from many people. As such there are people we would like to acknowledge and thank.

There are a few people we want to particularly mention who have been especially helpful on our journey for this book, but also have contributed to the development of ACC. First, thanks to Paul Flaxman and Frank Bond – it was their pioneering work in the area of bringing ACT out of the therapy room and into the workplace that set the scene for ACC. Their innovations and commitment to research is inspiring.

A big thanks also to the practitioners whose work in developing ACC has guided and encouraged us, including Rachel Collis, Rob Archer, Russ Harris, Lee Hulbert-Williams, Nick Hulbert-Williams, Rachael Skews, Tim Anstiss and Richard Blonna.

If you have had any contact at all with the Association of Contextual Behavioral Science (ACBS; the international body within which ACT sits), you will appreciate what a wonderfully sharing and cooperative organisation this is. Prosocial values are at the forefront, guiding both the organisation and the individuals who make it up. We want to give a massive thank you the ACBS community for everything they have offered us in terms of support, ideas and commitment.

Part I

THE DISTINCTIVE THEORETICAL FEATURES OF ACC

1

The world according to ACC

For many coachees, especially those in the business world, the Acceptance and Commitment Coaching (ACC) approach feels like a radical departure. They, like almost all of us, have been raised to believe a number of things about life and how to navigate it. For instance, one overwhelmingly popular belief – if not always expressed in exactly these terms – is that the key to fulfilment in life is to avoid discomfort and pursue "happiness". When an attempt is made to define what is meant by happiness, it is normally described as a state where pleasant feelings and thoughts outnumber unpleasant feelings and thoughts.

A further belief – one that is popular in the Western world in general, but particularly fuels the worlds of business and sport – is that the achievement of "success" is the most reliable means of banishing unpleasant internal experiences and achieving happiness. In this context, success is often equated with status, influence, material reward and affirmation and esteem from others.

You can see how the combination of these two beliefs can tie people up in knots: perpetually chasing a definition of success almost entirely defined by factors external to the self, in pursuit of a state – "happiness" – which is by its nature ephemeral.

The ACC philosophy, while sometimes exploring ideas of the self and involving the kind of meditative exercises that can initially be met with scepticism, is determinedly pragmatic. It posits that uncomfortable, unwanted thoughts and feelings are an inevitable part of life; indeed, that a life that is fully lived, rich, fun and fulfilling will necessarily involve willingly exposing oneself to this stuff. It also acknowledges that, as human beings, we are pretty much hard-wired to avoid unpleasant internal events. This natural inclination, and its limitations as a means of navigating through life, is beautifully captured in the story of "The Bear and the Blueberry Bush".

Imagine you are following a path through a forest. You have been following the path for several hours and you are not 100% sure where you are going. Already on the journey there have been some really cool, fun moments – things you've seen that have been weird and beautiful. But there have been some unpleasant moments too – stuff that has been scary, and at times you've felt completely lost. Right now you know that you are a little bit tired and very hungry ...

Then you come to a fork in the path – it splits off in two directions. When you look down one path you see, bathed in sunlight, a tall, lush, wild blueberry bush. When you look down the other path you see, snarling from the shadows, an enormous, hulking, grizzly bear. Which path do you choose?

Naturally, almost everybody who considers this question will choose the path with the blueberry bush. It's no more than common sense from an evolutionary perspective. We have evolved to avoid things that are or feel threatening, while moving towards those that offer safety and security and nourishment. This has helped us to survive and prosper as a species, and remains a helpful guiding principle when applied to the external world. But it becomes a trap when we apply it too rigidly to our internal worlds – the world of thoughts, feelings, memories and sensations. If we always avoid situations that are challenging, a bit scary or that take us out of our comfort zones, our lives become very limited. Sure, it works in the short term – there is a sense of relief in not having to put up with those horrible thoughts and feelings. But in the long term?

Nothing changes. You don't connect, you don't do the stuff that matters most, you don't grow or develop or push yourself.

The role of the ACC coach is to propose to our coachees that it is not the presence of unwelcome thoughts and feelings that is problematic and that derails us in life, it is the way that we tend to respond to them. It is the impulse to push them away, deny them, struggle with them or avoid situations in which they might be evoked that keeps us stuck. In addition to this, our role is then to help them develop their *psychological flexibility*.

Psychological flexibility is the ability to fully connect with the present moment in order to engage behavioural patterns supporting movement towards valued ends. It is comprised of six processes: *acceptance, defusion, contact with the present moment, self-as-context, values* and *committed action*. These processes are set out visually in a hexagon, also known as the Hexaflex (see Figure 1.1).

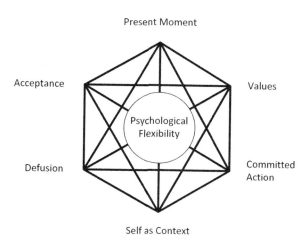

Figure 1.1 The ACT Hexaflex

As coaches we will be working with people who want more from their lives in some way – where they are now is not where they want to be. Perhaps they want to develop as leaders at work; perhaps they want to forge a new career entirely; perhaps they want to improve their performance in a sport or physical pursuit; perhaps they want to find a better balance between work life and personal life. For them, changing will mean stepping into the unknown, and doing that is bound to provoke some challenging or uncomfortable thoughts and feelings. The ACC approach is to consider these thoughts and feelings entirely normal and healthy. Indeed, they can be seen as "the price of admission" to a life that is rich, fulfilling, fun, challenging and fully lived. As you will see, a growing body of research suggests that helping coachees to develop their psychological flexibility is a proven, effective way of enabling them to consciously move towards their goals and values.

2

Why ACC?

From being a relatively uncommon intervention only a couple of decades ago, coaching is now a well-established discipline in multiple areas. Health and wellness coaching, career coaching and, in particular, business and executive coaching are rapidly growing in terms of popularity and professional credibility. A 2016 study by the International Coach Federation (ICF) estimated that there were approximately 53,000 professional coach practitioners worldwide, with a global revenue from coaching of over US$2 billion per year.

This rapid growth is based on an emerging body of anecdotal and research evidence attesting to the effectiveness of coaching. On this basis, what is the need for ACC? Isn't the coaching world doing fine without it? Perhaps, but along with the growing profile of coaching will continue to come a growing necessity for regulation, professionalism and scientific rigour. As we will explain in Chapter 4 (ACT coaching research), this is an area where ACC offers something that is absent elsewhere in the coaching world.

Fillery-Travis and Lane (2006) concluded that answering the question "does it work?" is no longer enough, and that it is now time to shift to "*how* does it work?". While one of the strengths of the coaching approach has been its willingness to borrow and learn from other models and psychological disciplines, the fact is that this means that most coaches are not using theoretically consistent techniques or measures. As a result, the question "how does it work?" has not been satisfactorily answered.

ACC has an answer. Pioneered by the likes of Rachel Skews, Rachel Collis, Richard Blonna, Rob Archer and Tim Anstiss, ACC is based on the principles of Acceptance and Commitment Therapy (ACT). As such, it has a clear theoretical underpinning through which we can understand the underlying mechanisms and processes of any change that occurs. The focus is clearly on how language and thinking influence human behaviour, and how the development of psychological flexibility can enable coachees to make significant and sustainable steps in the direction of their values. This coherent model of human behaviour means that there is a clarity and consistency to coaching sessions in terms of context and focus, if not content and structure.

Indeed, the theoretical basis offers a clear and robust framework within which the coach can exercise creativity and collaborate freely with their coachee. ACC is by its nature experiential, which lends it to interesting, engaging coaching interactions. Many find it to be a refreshing departure from the highly verbal counselling style of interaction that many expect or have experienced previously in coaching.

Here, the underlying theory of Relational Frame Theory (see Chapter 3, Relational Frame Theory for dummies) actually informs the nature of the coaching interaction, in that it emphasises direct, experiential learning over verbal instruction. This promotes the use of creative exercises, metaphors and interactions that are designed to enrich coachees' understanding of their inner worlds and the interaction between their behaviour and the outside world. As a result, there is often an added level of dynamism and experiential immersion to the coaching interaction.

Perhaps surprisingly, given that it has its roots in clinical practice, ACT is uniquely suited to coaching, and the transition to ACC has been simple. It is based on language-based learning processes fundamental to all human functioning, rather than a model of deficit or disability. Simply put, the assumption is that the coachee is not broken, in need of fixing, but simply struggling with the way that we as humans tend to respond to the language-machine of the mind. It is this struggle that underpins any problem that a coachee might be experiencing. Coaches often refer to themselves as process, rather than content experts. A coach doesn't need to be an expert in the field their coachee works in or the area in which they wish to make change; their role is simply to facilitate and promote this process of change. The versatile nature of ACC is perfectly suited to this. It doesn't matter what issue the coachee presents with, or what industry they work in. The ACC coach's job is simply to help them develop their psychological flexibility, and we can trust that values-based change will follow.

Which brings us to the final point we would wish to make in addressing the question "why Acceptance and Commitment Coaching?". The model itself is inherently humanistic, compassionate and optimistic. It is based on the assumption that as human beings each of us has a set of values, a core purpose; one that can get lost in the swirl of thoughts, feelings and judgements that are an inevitable part of the human experience. And yet, even when these thoughts seem overwhelming, when the feelings seem unbearable, it is possible to connect with these values and take action to live a life of meaning. At its best, ACC is not just effective in terms of behaviour change, it is personally empowering and ennobling.

References

Fillery-Travis, A., & Lane, D. (2006). Does coaching work or are we asking the wrong question? *International Coaching Psychology Review, 1*, 23–35.

International Coaching Federation. (2016). ICF global coaching study. Retrieved from https://coachfederation.org/app/uploads/2017/12/2016ICFGlobalCoachingStudy_ExecutiveSummary-2.pdf

3

Relational Frame Theory for dummies

Learning to play an instrument normally happens through a combination of instruction by someone else and practice. Eventually you become competent and may even master your instrument. In learning, it's not a requirement to know how to read sheet music, but it can dramatically open up different ways of learning new pieces of music and ways to play your instrument. This is how Relational Frame Theory (RFT) fits into ACC. We would propose that a good understanding of ACT is plenty good enough for 90% of coaching situations. But to expand your practice, it's helpful to have an understanding to the fundamentals behind the model.

A significant proportion of modern psychological approaches has its roots in behaviourism, an approach pioneered by the famous and famously named Burrhus Frederic Skinner. At its heart, behaviourism said that every action we take is dependent on previous actions and their consequences. If the consequences of an action were not so good, the behaviour became less likely to be repeated. If they were good, it became more likely. This describes the principle of *reinforcement* within a framework of learning called *operant conditioning.* These principles have enormous applicability to every sphere of human activity.

The one arena that behaviourism and Skinner failed to crack was that most important area of *languaging.* This is the very activity you are engaging in right now – making sense of these funny scratchy inky symbols, stamped onto sheets of paper or electronic device, as we attempt, using these symbols, to communicate to you in a meaningful way. Language allows us to communicate our desires and wishes efficiently without relying on random hoots and grunts. It gives us a way to recall events from the past. It allows us the tools to anticipate the future. Collectively, it hugely increases our opportunity to cooperate, on a scale seldom seen in the natural world.

Skinner had attempted to provide an account of human verbal behaviour (Skinner, 1957), but was heavily criticised for not being able to address one of its key features, its generativity (Chomsky, 1959). Generativity accounts for the explosion of language learning that happens with infants. It's nearly as if they come pre-programmed to learn language, and in a certain way they do. While Skinner's behavioural principles were unable to account for emergent (untrained or derived) responses, RFT does (Hayes, Barnes-Holmes & Roches, 2001).

RFT proposes that our language abilities are learned and we learn to relate objects, concepts or ideas to each other. This type of learning is known as *arbitrarily applicable derived relational responding*. At its core, it states that we learn to relate objects, concepts or ideas to each other using different "frames". Frames can include "same" (this book is the same as that book) or "different" (I am different from you). Frames can also relate using time (now or then) and space (here or there). We can frame events mutually; for example, the sun is bigger than the moon, which, in this context, confers largeness on to the sun, and smallness on to the moon. But, given a cue, we can relate in combination; the galaxy is larger than the sun and the moon. This relating ability becomes so fluent and easy that, except with heavy-duty drugs or more than healthy amounts of alcohol, it almost never switches off.

Typically, we start deriving relations between objects' non-arbitrary properties (an apple is bigger than a grape), but we quickly we move into arbitrary qualities that we all just decide to agree on (this scruffy, dirty £50 note is worth more than that bright, shiny £1 coin). But sometimes the relations we derive may not be fact based or even agreed upon (you are a better human being than me).

So, in summary, this ability to derive relations from anything to anything is an incredibly handy tool. But it does come with a dark side. There are three ways this occurs.

The first is that we become incredibly reliant on this ability, which across many contexts allows us to effectively solve and fix a wide array of problems. This takes us down a path where our go-to solution is to consult with our minds. Which is great, when it works. But when it doesn't, it's terrible. The standard solution to something we don't like is to move away from it. We encounter a loud, scary noise and we run fast in the opposite direction. When the thing we don't like is located within us (such as a memory or a thought or a feeling), things get sticky very quickly. Experience says, "I can't run from my thoughts/feelings/ memories – they're in me, they're part of me". A problem solving mind says, "fix it/solve it/remove it/get rid of it" etc. You can begin to see the problem. This issue quickly amplifies when we find we're not able to "solve" the problem. Suddenly it becomes "I" that is the problem, which leads to all sorts of deep and treacherous rabbit holes.

Second, as we're engaging in the relentless deriving of rela-tions, we abstract ourselves away from the direct experience right in front us. This can mean we deprive ourselves of useful information that sits outside of what we already know. It makes us far less sensitive to feedback and the contingencies around us, and therefore far less curious, creative and psychologically flex-ible. This is how we can make ourselves afraid of experiences we've never had (ever had the fear of starting a new role after a promotion?). Or how we miss important opportunities for change when everything says we should make the change (like when we don't clear the big, important tasks off our desk at the start of the day, even when our experience repeatedly tells us that leaving them to the last minute at the end of the day makes it 10 times harder).

Finally, we can easily confuse the non-arbitrary with arbi-trary. This goes someway to explaining why negative thoughts pack such a punch. You can hear it when coachees talk: "I work in marketing for a construction company (fact), I've been there over 10 years (fact) and I'm a terrible manager (fact?)". Of course, this may be an actual fact, but notice what happens when we treat all language as equal; it becomes much harder to disentangle fact from fiction.

All of this has direct relevance to coaching sessions. When we are working to understand points at which coachees are particularly stuck, we would do well to consider some of the ways that language may be trapping them. Helping them to see these subtle, yet powerful traps is crucial to developing alternative, more flexible ways of responding and therefore ways that facilitate more effective responding.

References

Chomsky, A. N. (1959). A review of Skinner's verbal behavior. *Language*, *35*, 26–58.

Hayes, S. C., Barnes-Holmes, D., & Roche, B. (Eds) (2001). *Relational Frame Theory: A Post-Skinnerian Account of Human Language and Cognition*. New York: Plenum Press.

Skinner, B. F. (1957). *Verbal Behavior*. Acton, MA: Copley Publishing Group.

4

ACT coaching research

The evidence

As a profession, coaching is relatively new and as such, encounters the issues a burgeoning field is exposed to as it matures, such as accreditation, regulation and identity issues (Page & de Haan, 2014). Therefore, as would be expected, outcome data have been later to develop, particularly higher quality randomised controlled trials, although in the last 10 years, a number have been published. So, what do the data say so far? At this point, there is a developing body of literature to suggest that coaching interventions do in fact have a wide range of positive benefits. In an informal review, Grant, Cavanagh, Parker and Passmore (2010), identified 11 randomised controlled trials (RCTs) of coaching interventions, the majority of which were solution focused and/ or cognitive behavioural in type. The authors concluded that these studies suggested that coaching could have a positive impact on outcomes such as performance and well-being. In a subsequent formal meta-analysis of 18 RCTs, Grant (2017) found that individual coaching had positive effects on performance, well-being, coping, work attitudes and goal attainment. It was concluded that attention now needed to shift to identify a theoretical framework to help understand these results so that underlying mechanisms and processes could be identified.

Overview of ACT data

To date, over 200 RCTs have explored the effectiveness of ACT with a wide variety of issues, including work stress, mood problems, anxiety, substance misuse and serious mental health conditions (Boorman, Morris, & Oliver, 2017). In meta-analyses, ACT has been shown to be at least as effective as established protocols such as cognitive behavioural therapy (A-Tjak et al., 2015; Öst, 2014; Smout, Hayes, Atkins, Klausen, & Duguid, 2012).

ACT has been adapted for non-clinical working populations, and developed into brief, skills-focused interventions (e.g., Bond & Flaxman, 2006; Brinkborg, Michanek, Hesser, & Berglund, 2011; Flaxman & Bond, 2010; Flaxman, Bond, & Livheim, 2013). A number of RCTs have demonstrated significant positive results on well-being, stress, burn out and general mental health (e.g., Bond & Bunce, 2000; Brinkborg et al., 2011; Frogeli, Djordjevic, Rudman, Livheim, & Gustavsson, 2016; Lloyd, Bond, & Flaxman, 2013; McConachie, McKenzie, Morris, & Walley, 2014).

A cluster of studies have now looked at the links between psychological flexibility and performance outcomes. To date, psychological flexibility has been found to predict employee innovation (Bond & Bunce, 2000), new skill learning (Bond & Flaxman, 2006) and higher perceived job control, and subsequent mental health and reduced absenteeism rates (Bond, Flaxman, & Bunce, 2008).

In total, the evidence points to a strong association between psychological flexibility, workplace well-being and performance outcomes (see Hayes, Luoma, Bond, Masuda, & Lillis, 2006 for a review).

Given these positive results, it's perhaps not surprising to see ACT being taken into sports coaching and there are now several studies showing some good emerging evidence for the efficacy of these procedures. The most comprehensively developed is the Mindfulness, Acceptance and Commitment (MAC) programme by Frank Gardiner and Zella Moore (Gardiner & Moore, 2007). The MAC programme has taken ACT into the sporting arena, using acceptance, mindfulness procedures, along with values-based actions towards performance-supporting behaviours.

In addition to a series of published case studies, there are now three published trials reporting effective outcomes for the MAC programme. These include increased mental health and coach-rated performance outcomes for female athletes (Gross et al., 2016), improved coach-rated performance in hockey and volleyball players Wolanin & Schwanhausser, 2010) and reductions in injury rates for soccer/football players (Ivarsson, Johnson, Andersen, Fallby, & Altemyr, 2015).

Bernier, Thienot, Codron, and Fournier (2009) used a mindfulness and acceptance protocol, blending mindfulness-based cognitive therapy (MBCT) with ACT in an open trial with a group of seven elite golfers. All golfers in the intervention condition improved both their standing in national rankings, and also improved their performance on predefined behavioural outcomes.

Outside of the sporting arena, two studies found that ACT interventions successfully increased chess players' performance (Ruiz & Luciano, 2012) and improved performance of musicians experiencing performance-related anxiety (Juncos et al., 2017).

To date, there has only been one formal evaluation of an ACT coaching intervention. Skews (2018) carried out an RCT in which 127 participants were randomly allocated to receive an intervention (three 1.5 hour ACT-based coaching sessions) or a control condition. Participants were all civil service middle managers. The intervention consisted of values-based goals setting, mindfulness practice and defusion and acceptance exercises. The results showed significant effects on proactivity, well-being, self-efficacy and goal achievement. Increases were also found in psychological flexibility, which was found to mediate well-being and self-efficacy.

Summary

In summary, although the data are limited, there is good emerging support for the use of coaching interventions for a wide range of outcomes. What has been missing, however, is a solid theoretical model that outlines processes from which to understand the outcomes seen. ACT has the ability to do this: it has a very clearly explicated model of change that is broad in scope, to include not only health and well-being outcomes, but importantly extends into key areas for coaching, such as performance. Research outcomes from the broader literature warrant some degree of excitement when thinking about the application to coaching. Although data exploring ACT within a coaching context are in their infancy, there is cause for optimism as we see positive benefits across a wide variety of settings, with a broad range of outcomes.

References

A-Tjak, J. G., Davis, M. L., Morina, N., Powers, M. B., Smits, J. A., & Emmelkamp, P. M. (2015). A meta-analysis of the efficacy of acceptance and commitment therapy for clinically relevant mental and physical health problems. *Psychotherapy and Psychosomatics, 84,* 30–36.

Bernier, M., Thienot, E., Codron, R., & Fournier, J. F. (2009). A multistudy investigation examining the relationship between mindfulness and acceptance approaches and sport performance. *Journal of Clinical Sports Psychology, 3,* 320–333.

Bond, F. W., & Bunce, D. (2000). Mediators of change in emotion-focused and problem-focused worksite stress management interventions. *Journal of Occupational Health Psychology, 5,* 156–163.

Bond, F. W., & Flaxman, P. E. (2006). The ability of psychological flexibility and job control to predict learning, job performance, and mental health. *Journal of Organizational Behavior Management, 26,* 113–130.

Bond, F. W., Flaxman, P. E., & Bunce, D. (2008). The influence of psychological flexibility on work redesign: Mediated moderation of a work reorganization intervention. *Journal of Applied Psychology, 93,* 645–654.

Boorman, J., Morris, E., & Oliver, J. (2017). Acceptance and commitment therapy. In C. Feltham, & I. Horton (Eds), *The SAGE Handbook of Counselling and Psychotherapy*, 4th edition. Los Angeles: Sage Publications Ltd.

Brinkborg, H., Michanek, J., Hesser, H., & Berglund, G. (2011). Acceptance and commitment therapy for the treatment of stress among social workers: A randomized controlled trial. *Behaviour Research and Therapy*, *49*, 389–398.

Flaxman, P. E., & Bond, F. W. (2010). Worksite stress management training: Moderated effects and clinical significance. *Journal of Occupational Healthy Psychology*, *15*, 347–358.

Flaxman, P. E., Bond, F. W., & Livheim, F. (2013). *Mindful and Effective Employees: A Training Program for Maximizing Employee Well-being and Effectiveness Using Acceptance and Commitment Therapy*. Oakland, CA: New Harbinger.

Frogeli, E., Djordjevic, A., Rudman, A., Livheim, F., & Gustavsson, P. (2016). A randomized controlled pilot trial of acceptance and commitment training (ACT) for preventing stress-related ill health among future nurses. *Anxiety, Stress and Coping: An International Journal*, *29*, 202–218.

Gardiner, F. L., & Moore, Z. E. (2007). *The Psychology of Enhancing Human Performance: The Mindfulness-Acceptance-Commitment (MAC) Approach*. New York: Springer Publishing.

Grant, A. (2017). Coaching as evidence-based practice: The view through a multiple-perspective model of coaching research. In T. Bachkirova, G. Spence, & D. Drake (Eds), *The SAGE Handbook of Coaching*. Los Angeles: Sage Publications Ltd.

Grant, A., Cavanagh, M., Parker, H., & Passmore, J. (2010). The state of play in coaching today: A comprehensive review of the field. In G. P. Hodgkinson, & J. K. Ford (Eds), *International Review of Industrial and Organisational Psychology*. Chichester: Wiley-Blackwell Publishing.

Gross, M., Moore, Z. E., Gardner, F. L., Wolanin, A. T., Pess, R., & Marks, D. R. (2016). An empirical examination comparing the mindfulness-acceptance-commitment approach and psychological skills training for the mental health and sport performance of female student athletes. *International Journal of Sport and Exercise Psychology, 16*, 431–451. DOI: 10.1080/1612197X.2016.1250802

Hayes, S. C., Luoma, J., Bond, F., Masuda, A., & Lillis, J. (2006). Acceptance and commitment therapy: Model, processes, and outcomes. *Behaviour Research and Therapy*, *44*, 1–25.

Ivarsson, A., Johnson, U., Andersen, M. B., Fallby, J., & Altemyr, M. (2015). It pays to pay attention: A mindfulness-based program for injury prevention with soccer players. *Journal of Applied Sport Psychology*, *27*, 319–334.

Juncos, D. G., Heinrichs, G. A., Towle, P., Duffy, K., Grand, S. M., Morgan, M. C., Smith, J. D., & Kalkus, E. (2017). Acceptance and commitment therapy for the treatment of music performance anxiety: A pilot study with student vocalists. *Frontiers in Psychology*, *8*, 986.

Lloyd, J., Bond, F. W., & Flaxman, P. E. (2013). Identifying the psychological mechanisms underpinning a cognitive behavioural intervention for emotional burnout. *Work & Stress*, *27*, 181–199.

McConachie, D. A. J., McKenzie, K., Morris, P. G., & Walley, R. M. (2014). Acceptance and mindfulness-based stress management for support staff caring for individuals with intellectual disabilities. *Research in Developmental Disabilities*, *35*, 1216–1227.

Öst, L. G. (2014). The efficacy of acceptance and commitment therapy: An updated systematic review and meta-analysis. *Behaviour Research and Therapy*, *61*, 105–121.

Page, N., & de Haan, E. (2014). Does executive coaching work? *The Psychologist*, *27*, 582–587.

Ruiz, F. J., & Luciano, C. (2012). Improving international level chess-players' performance with an acceptance-based protocol. *The Psychological Record*, *62*, 447–461.

Skews, R. A. (2018). Acceptance and Commitment Therapy (ACT) Informed Coaching: Examining Outcomes and Mechanisms of Change. (Unpublished doctoral dissertation). Goldsmiths, University of London, London, UK.

Smout, M. F., Hayes, L., Atkins, P. W. B., Klausen, J., & Duguid, J. E. (2012). The empirically supported status of acceptance and commitment therapy: An update. *Clinical Psychologist*, *16*, 97–109.

Wolanin, A. T., & Schwanhausser, L. A. (2010). Psychological functioning as a moderator of the MAC-approach to performance enhancement. *Journal of Clinical Sport Psychology*, *4*, 312–322.

DISTINCTIVE THEORETICAL FEATURES OF ACC

5

Philosophy 101 for coaches

Functional contextualism

Whether explicitly stated or implicit, every scientific approach is undergirded by a philosophy that sets the stall out for making clear what is important to science and how knowledge is accumulated. Modern science commonly identifies with a form of *positivism*, which broadly states that science is the gathering of facts, and as more facts are gathered, the more closely we approach reality.

The *functional contextual* approach differs from a positivist approach in that those things that are *true* (aka facts) are only those that are known to work. Workability is specifically defined within this psychological framework as processes that move the person, team or organisation towards a predefined set of values. This means that to know what works, or is functional, requires knowledge of the context within which events occur. This pragmatic analysis identifies any contextual variables as potential targets for intervention and therefore clarifies why ACC focuses on changing the relationship an individual has with internal content, rather than seeking to change the actual content itself. This philosophy is baked in to the whole of the model and has a whole host of practical implications.

Let's set out an example to illustrate what we mean. Imagine one of your work colleagues starts acting in a distant and cold way towards you. Normally she's warm and friendly so you start to think if you've said or done something to offend her. Just as you really start to worry, she approaches you over lunch and suddenly bursts out in floods of tears. In between big sobs, she manages to say that her father recently died very suddenly. A shift in the context *dramatically* changes the effect (or functions) of her behaviour. It's probably fair to say that most of us don't spend our days pondering philosophy. But this example gives an illustration how the philosophical lens underpinning ACT, *functional contextualism*, can filter everyday life.

At its heart, it positions the context as crucial to gaining an understanding of how events impact or effect each other (i.e. their function). In the above example, the initial context functioned to create a degree of anxiety and criticism. As your colleague made her disclosure, the context dramatically changed, as did the functions.

ACT uses functional contextualism as its foundation for all subsequent endeavours. Rather than attempting to uncover the fundamental truths of all things, ACT aims to predict and influence human behaviour in ways that are useful and workable. This means that a behaviour isn't either inherently good or bad – to evaluate it, you need to know the context. For example, we would argue that there is nothing inherently good or bad about drinking alcohol. A glass of wine or two on a romantic evening out – that's a good thing (if that's what you're into of course). That same glass of wine or two, Monday morning on the drive to work before dropping the kids off at school, is probably a little less of a good thing.

This also effects the stance of ACT and this is very much relevant for coaching. If the presence of a thought or behaviour isn't actually good or bad in and of itself, it suggests that the thought or behaviour is not really the issue. It's then more the response to it that's key. Within ACC, we become deeply curious about not just how thoughts, feelings and behaviours *look* but how they *work* for our coachees. Or, put another way, how they work to help move our coachees towards the things that matter to them. And more than that, we seek to engender that same level of curiosity in them.

From this philosophical stance, we can move up a level to think about our basic behavioural principles. These state that learning occurs as a result of consequences. Behaviour that is followed by a consequence that is rewarding in some way is more likely to occur in future. And behaviour that's followed by something unpleasant or hurtful is typically less likely to happen. These aren't guarantees, just increased or decreased probabilities. But what's a reward and what's a punishment? Basic human fundamentals such as food and sex are usually rewarding. And things like pain tend to be punishing. But, sometimes food and sex can be punishing. And sometimes pain can be, well, rewarding. It all depends on what you're into. And of course, it all depends on the context to tell us how events work or function.

We have a saying in ACT that is "what works is what's true". This is very much a pragmatic way of looking at the world and pushes us to think about function over form. In a coaching session this could mean we ask questions like:

When you have the thought that colleagues are working harder than you, do you find it's easier or harder to take action towards what's important?

It's certainly true that working longer hours can sometimes mean you get more done, but what's that in the service of?

Notice the thought here – you're at the limit of your performance. What if you were to disengage from that and take a step back? What possibilities begin to open up?

In the above examples, we aim to help the coachee notice how the context (i.e. their relationship with thoughts or rules) supports taking these rules and thoughts very literally. We work to *play* with the context in order to notice new and interesting functions that may not have been quite so apparent before.

So in summary, functional contextualism isn't just an arcane pondering of angels on pin heads. It's deeply practical and drops right throughout the contextual behavioural science approach to land firmly in the middle of ACC to inform the coaching approach.

6

Defusion

In Chapter 3 we laid out the case of RFT and the proposition that language is both a good and a bad thing. On the one hand, it helps us communicate, store knowledge, anticipate threats and problem solve all sorts of things. On the other hand, language gives us the capacity to criticise, judge, worry and ruminate.

In our highly verbal society, it should come as no surprise that we tend to favour using language and thinking when it comes to solving problems. While thinking our way out of a problem is often an extraordinary talent to have, there are numerous scenarios where thinking is actually less helpful. Playing a complex piece of music on an instrument, having a difficult conversation with a team member who is upset, pushing at the edge of performance ("what if I get it wrong, this is not how I thought it would be, last time, it was better/worse/more/less"). In these examples, *experiencing* is required and a busy, worrying, problem-solving mind is likely to interfere with the task at hand, reducing psychological flexibility.

The term for the process whereby thinking interferes with psychological flexibility is *cognitive fusion*. Specifically, this is when we become fused with our thinking, so much so that direct experienced environmental consequences no longer exert any impact on behaviour. Our behavioural flexibility is greatly reduced, restricting or preventing movements towards chosen values. The term fusion is a metaphor for being fused with our thoughts, thinking or language. Just as if we were poured in together with the thinking products of our minds. Or as if our thoughts were welded on to us with absolutely no space or separation whatsoever.

Notice that fusion implies a *relationship* with our thinking in that *we* become *fused* with thought. This helps more clearly illuminate the problem, which is not in fact the mere presence of thinking, but in our *relationship* with thought. When fused with thinking, we treat thoughts very seriously, as if they are *truths* or rules that must be followed or obeyed. Thoughts become threatening, commanding and require immediate action. When we alter our relationship with our thoughts to *de-fuse*, other qualities surface. Thoughts need not be taken so seriously, they may need to be followed, but not necessarily. They may be true, but they may not be. They become far less commanding, threatening and demanding of immediate action. When fused, we are metaphorically connected to our thoughts; with defusion, we are separated, so there is space between us and our thoughts. In this space, there is more room to consider other guides to behaviour, such as our values.

Commonly, we evaluate thoughts by their correspondence with reality. That is, are our thoughts real, accurate or true? "I am late for work", "it's raining out, I need an umbrella", "my phone's battery is about to die" are all thoughts that lend themselves well to a veracity check. Thoughts such as "no-one else is ever late, they're better than me", "it's raining out, I'll catch a cold and die" or "my phone battery is about to die – yet another example of how the universe has it in for me" are, of course, not so easily checked out. In fact, engaging with such thoughts is likely to lead to worry, rumination and negativity. Defusion offers an alternative way to evaluate such thoughts, which is their workability, or, in other words, how well does buying such a thought help in taking effective action?

In coaching, it is common to work with coachees who come from environments that emphasise accuracy, being right and finding correct solutions, or where the coachees have been highly reinforced for successfully using their intellect.

Therefore, the focus in ACC is not necessarily changing the content of thoughts, but more on changing the context around which thinking is occurring. This will feel counterintuitive at first to coaching coachees, particularly those who strongly emphasise positive thinking (or the absence of negative thinking) as intrinsically linked to action. Of course, thoughts and actions are linked, but often it's a much more complex relationship that is seldom directly causal. Coachees can spend a lot of energy attempting to eliminate negative thoughts, whilst many opportunities for effective action pass them by. By defusing, thoughts and actions are de-coupled and deliberate choice of effective actions is more likely to occur.

Cognitive fusion is a technical term and when working with coachees, we tend to favour phrases like "hooked by your mind", "caught up in mind stuff", "bought what your mind's told you". You can get a sense here of how the metaphorical language conveys unhelpful entanglement with language. Of course it's possible to become unhelpfully fused with any thought, but the kinds that are likely to be most relevant to coaching sessions are:

- Fused with thoughts about the past or future (ruminating about past mistakes or worrying about events in the future)
- Fused with judgements about ourselves and others
- Fused with rules about how life should be ("you shouldn't act in that way")
- Fused with reasons ("I can't perform because I always screw up")
- Fused with thoughts about the self ("I'm not a good person; I'm not good enough")

A good example we often use to set the scene involves asking coachees to consider a significant achievement in their lives. And then to think back to the early stages of the journey and what thoughts were present. Typically, this will involve a mix – some of excitement and anticipation, but others of fear of failure and concerns about their abilities. All of course entirely natural. But if the presence of such thoughts were used as a guide to action, then not much action would ever occur! This example illustrates how it's not the thoughts themselves that are important – it's the response to them that's crucial. Defusing from them, seeing thoughts as thoughts, transitory pieces of verbal behaviour that will come and go, that may or may not be important, radically changes the context within which thoughts occur. Suddenly there is room for something else within this space to start guiding behaviour, and it's here that an ACC coach will be looking to drop in values.

7

Acceptance

It's worth saying from the outset that acceptance is a technical term that here has a complex and subtle meaning, distinct from the everyday use of the word. Crucially it is important to emphasise the active nature of the process of acceptance, as the word itself can sometimes be taken as synonymous with giving up, or grimly submitting to the inevitability of a life of pain and frustration. On the contrary, the ACT interpretation of acceptance proposes that we acknowledge that uncomfortable thoughts and feelings are part of a fully lived life, and encourages the coachee to willingly come into contact with this stuff in service of their values. When we talk about acceptance in ACT we are referring to an active and ongoing, unfolding stance towards thoughts and feelings that promotes a reduction in unnecessary struggle.

Acceptance means reducing unworkable strategies, as these only worsen the issue. Identifying workable strategies is central, as is practising these, even when feeling the entirely natural pull back into responding in old, automatic ways.

The opposite of acceptance, from an ACT perspective, is experiential avoidance. Experiential avoidance refers to habitual or pervasive avoidance that causes a level of behavioural harm. Built into this definition is a functional element, which requires a context to be identified before an action is labelled as avoidant. The important context here is valued action and the degree to which experiential avoidance hinders steps towards values. So there's a good chance that a Netflix binge of your favourite show will probably contain a bit of experiential avoidance. But it's about the amount you do it and the degree it interferes with you doing the things that matter.

Experiential avoidance appears to be an important variable in understanding a range of human behaviours. Research has linked it to many problems areas such as anxiety, trauma, depression, general well-being and performance (see Chapter 4, ACT coaching research).

Supporting acceptance is the process of cognitive fusion and these two often go together. Along with the actual emotional experience itself sits an evaluation of the experience. Fusion with thoughts such as "I can't handle this" or "this showing up means something very bad about me" are contexts that are highly likely to support experiential avoidance of a difficult emotion. Defusion from such thoughts creates a context within which acceptance can occur.

In lay terms, acceptance often has an emotional tone, such as when used like, "I feel accepting towards this". In ACC terms, acceptance is much less about the emotional qualities and much more about the behavioural actions. Sometimes, the term *willingness* is substituted, because it's a word that captures that active stance towards emotions. We might ask, what are you willing to make room and space for in order that you can do this really important action? The emphasis is less about tolerating the emotion and more about a genuine and full embracing of the emotion, such that its ability to impact behaviour becomes greatly reduced. Note of course that this isn't saying that emotion is not important, of course it is. The stance is about creating more choiceful actions in the presence of emotions. At times this may call for a deliberate setting aside of the urge that is associated with an emotion. For example, if upon coming home tired and irritable to find your partner distraught after receiving bad news, it's likely to be beneficial to set your own emotional needs aside for a while so you can be available for your partner. Alternatively, if you experience a nagging annoyance every time your colleague subtly undermines your achievements in front of your manager, simply dismissing your feelings may not be the most helpful course of action.

This re-orientates us to the response to emotion as key, rather than only the presence of emotion itself. Underpinning this is the notion that emotion is not toxic or problematic in and of itself; it's the response that creates the problems. Synonymous with Kirk Strosahl are the words, "the problem is not the problem, the *solution* is the problem", suggesting our common, habitual *solutions* actually end up creating the *problem*, not the mere presence of an unwanted emotion.

To give an example, think about performance anxiety. Unless you don't have a pulse or you're a psychopath (and there is evidence to support this), you will have experienced anxiety related to a performance experience at some point in your life. Whether it's from public speaking (more feared by most people than death itself) or leaping on stage to entertain 10,000 of your fans, it's possible that at some point your mind will go something like, "hey, don't forget, everyone's watching you and they're ready to judge the HELL out of you". Anxiety increases and suddenly your mind tells you that anxiety means it's all going wrong! You can't have this feeling, you have to control it, but you can't, it's as if it's just getting worse!! It's nearly as if the more you try to get rid of it and berate yourself for having it in the first place, the bigger it gets.

The example above is the "why" for acceptance. Whatever the experience, fighting and struggling with it increases the probability it will become problematic. At its heart, acceptance is helping coachees to recognise the pragmatics of struggling, with a suggestion of willingness as a potential alternative tool to have in the toolkit.

We like to call this the "workability game" and we will explore this in more detail in Chapter 16. Here we are asking our coachees "does this strategy work?". It also helps to be clear on what "work" means. Does it always work? In which contexts? How about in the short term or long term? Does it help you to feel like you're making the choices?

Here's another example:

> With the prospect of a promotion, a coachee says, *"It's like I get hit with a sense of dread and in my mind, I'm saying I don't have what it takes. If I did, I wouldn't feel like this. And that's when I find myself pulling back, not throwing my hat in the ring. At one level I know I can do it and I want to, it's time for me to stretch my wings! But that feeling is too much sometimes; I can't stand it"*

In this example, it's evident that the coachee's stance towards the emotion (supported by fusion) is creating a context of threat. Threat creates experiential avoidance, leading to a missed opportunity to take a valued action. It also has the unintended consequence of reinforcing the sense of *dread* being important and something that must be attended to. An ACC coach would help the coachee to evaluate responses to dread in terms of workability, broadening it out from a simple metric of reduction to consider other factors, specifically if the strategies helped moves towards values.

The aim therefore is to move the coachee towards a position of recognising internal experiences for what they are, just as experiences, and not as they say they are.

8

Contact with present moment

A key skill within any coaching context is the ability to reduce automatic ways of responding and foster a sense of awareness of internal content (thoughts, feelings, emotions and memories) in a given moment, and the degree to which that drives behavioural responding. This requires developing an observational stance on this content from the present moment that has qualities of detachment and non-judgement. Although mindfulness meditation is one method through which to develop this ability, the ACC model helps to identify underlying processes, allowing for the flexible application of a variety of procedures.

The modern world – and especially the modern workplace – is synonymous with pace, productivity and momentum. While contacting the present moment doesn't necessarily involve practically stopping or even slowing down, there is a quality of pause and reflection that it promotes which is anathema to the relentless forward energy of modern life. Making this an attractive proposition to the coachee is fundamental to the success of ACC with a coaching population and we will unfold how to make it come to life in Chapter 20.

In the popular book, *Why Zebras Don't Get Ulcers* by Robert Sapolsky (1994), this question gets answered. To save yourself the cost of buying the book, the answer to this question is that it turns out that zebras are experts in staying in the present moment. This means that zebras can go from a state of extreme distress, after being chased by a predator, to being relatively calm and relaxed the instant the zebra is out of a threat zone. How is this possible? Well, one of the key differences is that zebras aren't equipped with a thinking mind that readily takes them out of the present moment. The zebra won't be plagued by trauma as its mind takes it back to the chase. Or crushing survivor guilt for having escaped when another of its *dazzle* (yes, that is the collective noun for a group of zebras) didn't make it. This is of course different for your average human.

Thinking about this functionally, of course the ability to plan into the future or learn from past experiences is extremely useful to us as a species, but at the same time comes with a price. The price is that we become seduced by the past and future we conceptualise for ourselves in such a way that it becomes incredibly easy to take these as literal truths. This means that we can end up ruminating on past failures to the exclusion of all other contradictory experiences. Or that we worry about future events that have not yet happened to us. In this way our ability to respond to the contingencies directly in front of us becomes greatly reduced. This can lead to us behaving in inflexible ways based on a narrow view of our past experience or how we imagine things will be in the future. Someone might therefore not take up new challenges because they see themselves as having always failed in the past and therefore predict that their future will be the same. While this could of course be true, basing action only on a conceptualised past or future becomes quite limiting in that it leads to repetitive and unhelpful behaviour cycles.

From an ACC perspective, when fusion and experiential avoidance is high, it is more likely that our present moment awareness will be rigid and inflexible. This can mean that our potential focus of attention becomes narrow as we seek to avoid stimuli that we find distressing or threatening. For example, leading up to a difficult conversation with a colleague following a big row, we might distract ourselves to avoid thinking about it. Equally it may be the case that our attention becomes fragmented as we equally struggle to maintain attention where it needs to be. Within ACC, the focus is on developing *flexible* attentional properties that pragmatically serve our purposes and help us move in valued directions.

Cultivating the ability to flexibly contact the present moment allows for more direct contact with actual contingencies. This may mean being more aware of resources or alternative options in the environment. For example, worrying about a future poor performance can easily limit useful actions in the present. A more present moment stance would take action, which could include preparing for the performance event by eliciting appropriate support from others or doing things to replenish mental and physical resources. Contacting the present moment also includes becoming more aware of internal thoughts and feelings as they are occurring in the moment. In this way it could be said that here we are cultivating better self-knowledge. This greater level of awareness broadly promotes less automatic and more choiceful responding.

Reference

Sapolsky, R. M. (1994). *Why Zebras Don't Get Ulcers: A Guide to Stress, Stress Related Diseases, and Coping*. New York: W.H. Freeman.

L

9

Self as context

An understanding of the self is something that philosophers, researchers, psychologists and scientists have struggled to understand and explain for as long as we've had the ability to consider the fact. It could indeed be argued that an understanding of the self is the holy grail of philosophy and psychology. Climbing down a notch or two from such lofty goals, ACC aims to shine a *pragmatic* light on this business of the self.

RFT brings something useful to the table as we work to understand a functional definition of the self. RFT describes the self as a product of our ability to engage in language and communicate with those around us. As infants, we slowly make a crucial discrimination as we become aware that we are distinct and separate from a primary caregiver, often our mothers. We begin to develop a sense of self that has wishes, desires and needs that are distinct from those around us. In doing so, we learn that we are encapsulated within our physical boundaries and our sense of self is located in space that is different and distinct from you over there. Gradually emerges an awareness of time so that we can discriminate ourselves now from ourselves then. All the while, this deictic self contains all these different component parts – our thoughts, memories, feelings, emotions and sensations. Gradually, a sense of self as a context or container within which all of these events occur emerges. In this way, this aspect of our self is distinct from these parts or content, which themselves are ever-changing and fluctuating. *Self as context*, however, is unchanging. This offers a perspective from which we can observe and notice our internal content without being engaged with it. Metaphorically, this sense of self is akin to the broader sky that holds and contains all the clouds, wind and weather. The weather fluctuates constantly, whilst the sky remains the same and is unchanged by whatever weather is present in that moment.

It is from this place of observing that we can recognise and discriminate between this sense of self that notices and observes and the ever-changing and evolving internal experience. This is sometimes referred to as the *observing self.*

By locating from this observing perspective and having a recognition of flux and change of this content we can legitimately make choices about our actions. In developing an awareness of a *self as context*, processes such as defusion, mindfulness and acceptance are strengthened. This means that the impact of our internal experiences is reduced and with this comes a corresponding increased opportunity to choose from the present moment and not from a conceptualised future or past.

In contrast to the psychological flexibility offered by contacting our observing self, over-attachment to our *self as content* or conceptualised self can greatly reduce flexibility. This aspect of self is a rigid network of verbal relations about ourselves, or to put it another way, our self-story. We all hold stories or narratives about ourselves, which invariably fail to capture our full complexity and diversity. But they work to help us get by in the world, so that we "know" ourselves in relation to others. These self-stories are built up over a lifetime of experiences and are both evaluative and predictive. Some may work well for us ("I'm a strong person") but some might not ("I'm a failure"). They can be particularly prevalent and powerful in the high-stakes theatre of the workplace, where opportunities for judgement and evaluation of the self and others are countless.

Problems can develop however when we become too rigid and attached to our self-stories. When we become too attached to "I'm a strong person", it doesn't easily allow us to respond flexibly when behaviours evaluated as "weak" occur. Similarly, a strong attachment to "I'm a failure" can preclude actions that are about success and striving, if they are needed. It doesn't take much to puncture the illusion of a deep, inherent self that is woven into you as much as the colour of your eyes. For example, if we were to ask you to describe yourself in a number of different scenarios, such as on a first date, singing karaoke on a wild night out, speaking at a loved one's funeral or at home on the weekend in your pyjamas, chances are the kind of description you give about yourself would likely be very different. Which of course is normal, healthy and as it should be.

Developing a sense of how we relate to our own stories helps us to "get eyes on" these parts of our experience to reduce their unhelpful impact. The aim is to move to a point of observing our self-stories without always engaging. The ACC focus is not on changing the self-story itself but the relationship that we have with it.

Overall the approach aims to help us hold our self-stories more lightly. In this way we can become more resilient and less buffeted by the experiences of life, both positive and negative. Our self-story becomes less important and de-emphasised as we take actions that are chosen and in line with our values. Although holding onto our self-stories tightly may provide us with a sense of certainty, safety and security, it can also limit us, as it restricts us from taking action.

The more lightly we hold these self-stories, the more agile we can become in taking the perspective of others. When we are wrapped up in our self-stories, it can be easy to fall into the trap of wanting to be right, sure and certain. All these things make it more difficult to flexibly take the perspective of another individual. Notice of course that what is not suggested here is that we completely abandon our own self-narratives, more that we are flexible in terms of how we respond to them. This also allows us to shift our perspectives in time to think back to previous experiences that perhaps fall outside of a dominant self-narrative. For every example of failure there will be no doubt an example of success, but these become obscured from awareness once the "failure" self-story falls into place.

10

Values

In simplest terms, one could see values as the answer to the question "why?". Why would someone willingly open up to and accept difficult feelings? Why would someone consciously observe and come into contact with uncomfortable thoughts? Why would someone mindfully connect with a present moment that might be challenging or scary? Why would someone invest the time and energy that it takes to develop these skills?

There are a number of very helpful definitions of values in ACT literature and beyond. The one that we chose for our book *ACTivate Your Life* was that values are "*chosen life directions*". When describing values to coachees, we might talk about "what is important to us and gives us a sense of purpose; the person we want to be and the things we want to stand for".

We alighted on our definition in *ACTivate* because it captures two fundamental qualities of values: 1) they are personally chosen; 2) they are directions rather than destinations. Let's investigate these two features in a little more detail.

Personally chosen

In an ACC context, values are things which – when acted on – bring you a personal sense of meaning, vitality or fulfilment. We sometimes illuminate what values are by contrasting them with what they are *not*, and it is important to distinguish between values and morals or ethics. Morals and ethics tend to be socially constructed and, while they may have been personally assimilated to a degree, they sit outside of the self. Also unhelpful from our perspective is that they tend to be quite rigid. In terms of morality and ethics things are either right or wrong, good or bad. It is these kinds of inflexible distinctions that lend themselves to cognitive fusion.

Directions rather than destinations

Another distinction that is helpful to make clear is between values and goals. This is especially important in the context of coaching as invariably people seek out coaching because there is something they want that they do not currently have. Often this is a concrete, tangible outcome of some kind – a new job, a promotion, better results at work, a relationship, the possibilities are endless. It may also be a more general desire for personal or professional development. While these outcomes are entirely noble, and the coach will endeavour to help the coachee achieve them, in ACC we have a strong focus on values.

We see values as being a reliable tool to navigate through life, and to ensure that not only are we moving consistently towards our goals, but towards the *right* goals – namely, values-based goals. For example, it would be entirely understandable for a work-based coachee to set themselves a goal around achieving a promotion. They could work towards that relentlessly and achieve it, but what if on the way they have ended up neglecting important values around being adventurous, creative or innovative. If values are sacrificed in pursuit of a goal, it will not feel satisfying or fulfilling when it is achieved.

A focus on values as well as goals not only means that goals are meaningful, it allows for much greater flexibility in terms of behavioural responding. For instance, a value of "being creative" can be expressed in any number of ways, in any number of contexts. A value of "caring for other people" can be acted on in any moment – making a partner a cup of tea, sending a text message to a parent, spending some time with a colleague who is down, or taking steps to shift to a career in the caring professions. All of these are entirely valid ways of expressing that value.

Our favourite metaphor here is to think of values as being like a compass guiding you through the journey of life. Taking conscious action on your values is like heading west – it's a direction you can head in, rather than a destination you will ever actually reach. Goals are like the sights you see or the places you visit as you travel – they are cool and fun and satisfying, and there is always further to go as you head west, towards your values.

Another distinction we make is between values and feelings or, more specifically, values and feeling *good*. There may be an expectation that following values will lead to "happiness" – an expectation that can lead to disappointment. While acting on values might well be accompanied by pleasant emotions, it is also likely to increase contact with stuff we care about, which can bring pain and difficult feelings. In ancient Greek philosophy the distinction was made between the psychological well-being that comes from flourishing, belonging, life purpose and personal growth (*eudaimonia*) and pleasure for its own sake (*hedonia*). ACC does not eschew *hedonia*, but actively promotes the longer-term well-being that is associated with *eudaimonia*.

The presence of pain can in fact be seen as an indicator that we are in touch with our values – usually painful emotion showing up is a sign that something we care about has been touched. This can be very helpful and reassuring for coachees, and promotes the capacity of willingness that is fundamental to psychological flexibility.

Reference

Oliver, J., Hill, J., & Morris, E. (2015). *ACTivate Your Life: Using Acceptance and Mindfulness to Build a Life that Is Rich, Fulfilling and Fun*. London: Constable & Robinson.

11

Committed action

In the previous chapter we described values as being like a compass: something to which we can refer to ensure that we are heading in the right direction in the journey of life. In that case, committed action is the process of mapping out the route and actually embarking on the journey – it is the behavioural component of valued living, where we turn our values from intentions and ideals into action.

It is also here that we help our coachees to experiment with the range of different ways that they can act on values. A manager with a core value of creativity could set herself an ambitious long-term goal of being promoted to a director position, from where she can make creativity, improvisation and innovation fundamental to the company's way of working. In addition to this, creativity can be incorporated into any moment, from the way she chairs a team meeting to the clothes she wears. This is crucial to a full understanding of committed action in the context of ACC. We are not just talking about the action taken towards specific goals that are part of a coaching action plan – equally important are the moment-by-moment decisions that can be taken in service of values at any time.

Given the goal and action focus of coaching, it may be tempting to view committed action as the endpoint or ultimate product of ACC. However, it is important to regard it more as a *part of the process*, building on and enriching the other core ACC processes. If the essential purpose of ACC is building psychological flexibility, committed action is about learning to be *mindful and flexible* in one's behaviour.

In taking values-based actions, coachees are going to come into contact with a range of internal experiences, some pleasant and some unpleasant. When the unpleasant or unwanted thoughts, feelings, memories or sensations show up we should encourage our coachees to view them as opportunities to practise defusion, acceptance and contact with the present moment, and to check in with their values as they consciously choose what course of action to pursue next. This is the point of committed action in the context of ACC: goals are not set to be charged towards relentlessly; mindfulness skills are not developed to simply push out of the way any obstacles that might arise as we move towards those goals. We set values-based goals and begin to move toward them consciously; then, as internal experiences that might be barriers to action arise, we use our mindfulness skills to manage them, so that we can make a conscious decision whether to persist in the current course of action or change tack, depending on which is most likely to be effective.

Ideally what this will mean for our coachees is that they achieve or exceed the goals that they aimed to work towards through coaching. But from an ACC perspective our aim is to help our coachees develop their psychological flexibility. Here what this means is supporting them in building larger and larger patterns of effective action. In developing their willingness to experience uncomfortable thoughts and feelings our coachees are able to experience the positive consequences of a new behaviour, increasing the likelihood that they will try it again. This positive reinforcement is a much more effective way of building patterns of effective behaviour than the negative reinforcement of experiential avoidance.

In Chapter 23 (Helping coachees take committed action) we will talk in more detail about ACC goal setting, and how to work with people to help them stay on track. But a point that is worth raising now is that the ACC approach to the pursuit of goals may be a little different than in other coaching contexts. In ACC we tend to focus on the process of taking action towards goals, rather than solely on the outcomes of those actions. This doesn't mean that we pay no attention to whether the coachee is making progress towards their goals – but it does mean that the goals we encourage them to set are clearly and explicitly related to their values, and that we judge "success" more on whether they took action in service of that value, rather than whether they got the result they were hoping for.

By relocating the metric for "success" away from outcomes (which are inevitably at least partly contingent on factors outside of the individual's control) and towards the process of consciously acting on values (which is entirely within the individual's control), the coachee can access a powerful sense of purpose and autonomy.

Again coachees experience the benefits of positive reinforcement, continually receiving affirmative feedback from their willingness to mindfully come into contact with uncomfortable internal experiences. At best this is the catalyst for the evolution of growing patterns of values-based action, and a developing capacity to consistently return to values regardless of how many times our coachees may drift from them. Not only that, it builds in them a sense of resilience – an awareness that even perceived failures can be accommodated as opportunities to learn, grow and continue to move in the direction of their values.

Part II

THE DISTINCTIVE PRACTICAL FEATURES OF ACC

12

What we talk about when we talk about ACC

If you are a coach thinking about incorporating ACC into your practice, you will need to be conscious about how you communicate about it with potential coachees. Whether you are explaining your way of working to an interested one-to-one coachee, or actively marketing to the Human Resources (HR) or Learning and Development department of an organisation, it pays to be succinct about what ACC actually *is*, and clear about the benefits of the approach.

While different individuals or organisations will have differing expectations about the precise "return on investment" they can expect from working with you, all will need their initial communication with you to give them a clear top-line understanding of the benefits of ACC. As practitioners, we may be personally compelled by the advantages of defusing from unhelpful thoughts, and the distinction between self as context and self as content, but our potential coachees may not be. Here, as our "elevator pitch", we favour clear, functional language. For example, we might say that ACC is about *"developing ways of taking more effective action in life by learning to respond more mindfully and skilfully to thoughts and emotions".*

We consciously use words like "effective" and "skilful". The intention is to make absolutely clear that there is an action focus to ACC, and that we are not interested in promoting "positive thinking" or changing emotions, simply managing them more *skilfully* so we can be more *effective.*

The idea of an "elevator pitch" is simply to open the door for further discussion, and the most important part of any initial contact with an individual or organisation will be listening. We can be confident that if we listen carefully to their specific needs and expectations, ACC is versatile enough that we can find a way of communicating about it that will speak to them.

However, there is a general rationale that we often refer to when explaining the benefits and relevance of ACC to the world we live in today. We talk about how the world is changing all the time, and modern life presents us with increasing challenges – an accelerating rate of innovation and development; pressure to deliver more, often with fewer resources; a linked-in world where technology can mean we are always connected to the workplace (and if not to the workplace, then to other sources of psychological stimulus). We cannot expect to thrive in this world with the same set of skills that guided us through the world as it once was. We need a new way of working to sit alongside those that have guided us this far. We propose that this new skillset is that of psychological flexibility.

A rationale such as this gives a sense of relevance and urgency, and makes the benefit of ACC clear without undermining the coachee's current strategies. As we have mentioned previously, the argument is that – in the words of Marshall Goldsmith (2008) – "what got you here might not get you there". The invitation is to "add another tool to your toolbox", in order to increase behavioural range, flexibility and choice.

With this as context, and a clear understanding of the coachee's needs, we can really start to communicate the unique benefits of the ACC approach. As outlined in Chapter 4 (ACT coaching research), there is an extensive evidence base to support the role of ACC interventions in increasing psychological flexibility and a clear association between psychological flexibility, workplace well-being and performance outcomes (see Hayes, Luoma, Bond, Masuda, & Lillis, 2006 for a review).

Most other coaching and training approaches do not have anything close to the quantity and quality of supporting evidence as ACT applied in a coaching context. Our suggestion would be that, while overselling this aspect is not necessary, coachees (especially in organisations) respond very well to being directed towards this supporting research.

Given that ACC is best delivered in a way that is experiential rather than didactic, giving a potential coachee an ACC-consistent experience is usually better than simply explaining it. Many coaches give individual coachees "taster" sessions, and it is entirely possible to do this for groups as well – perhaps a single session to be run during a lunch hour or after work. Our suggestion would be that these taster sessions involve one of the more memorable and accessible exercises, perhaps involving a physical metaphor. It could also be useful to incorporate one of these exercises into a meeting with potential training commissioners. An easy and illustrative one here might be the "two pieces of paper exercise" or "Flaxman manoeuvre" that we will describe in Chapter 15.

An experience like this is likely to be much more memorable than simply talking about ACC. Backed up by a clear thesis on the relevance and utility of ACC, along with plentiful supporting research evidence, you will have a strong case for why any individual or organisation should consider investing in you as an ACC coach.

References

Goldsmith, M. (2008). *What Got You Here Won't Get You There: How Successful People become Even More Successful.* London: Profile Books.

Hayes, S. C., Luoma, J., Bond, F., Masuda, A., & Lillis, J. (2006). Acceptance and commitment therapy: Model, processes, and outcomes. *Behaviour Research and Therapy, 44,* 1–25.

13

Assessment

The first session will focus on setting up the coaching work with your coachee and offers the opportunity to set expectations. This is your chance to do *active assessment*, which is comprised of three key components (see Figure 13.1): 1) relationship building, where the coach works to establish an effective working relationship with the coachee, 2) direction setting, where the coach and coachee set goals, and 3) information gathering, in which the coach draws out key information relevant to the goals. Each of these is held in mind throughout the first meeting and the coach moves interchangeably between them.

Relationship building

Good coaching relationships are built on a foundation of equality and common humanity. It's important for a coachee to know the coach has the skills to help, but also is able to understand the heart of the issue. As with any coaching assessment, we work hard to dial down the "expert" role as a coach, and dial up our role as a "facilitator of change". As such we often use the two mountains metaphor to make this relationship more explicit:

> *There's you on your mountain, climbing onwards and upwards. You've come here for help either with a particularly icy patch, or maybe you want to really push yourself to the next level. And here's me, over here, also on my mountain – not at the top, having gloriously conquered this fine peak, but working my way up,*

Figure 13.1 Active assessment

getting stuck on icy patches and also wanting to push myself and do well. What I'll be offering is a unique perspective, from my position here, on your journey, along with some ideas of specialist equipment and skills that might help for icy challenges or getting to the next level. This perspective, along with your hard won experience, is what we'll use to work as a team to help you get the most out of our time together.

In setting the relationship, it's always useful to address the issue of confidentiality. In our experience, most coachees are aware that issues discussed will be kept confidential, but an explicit statement by the coach reinforces this and sends a message that the coach is working for the coachee. This can

THE DISTINCTIVE PRACTICAL FEATURES OF ACC

be particularly important when coaching within workplace settings, when the employer may have commissioned the sessions. If there is an expectation that outcomes need to be reported back, this should be addressed at the very start.

Sometimes this may lead to situations where the coachee feels somewhat coerced to attend and motivation and readiness to change are low. This is good to identify early on and address (see Chapter 27 for ideas here).

Direction setting

It's important to convey the notion that ACC is active, and you will be helping the coachee set goals that are specifically linked to her or his values. Lots of good coaching models have this explicit active goal-setting component and ACC adds to this by bringing in *values*. To draw out goals, the following questions can be helpful:

- What would you like to see different as a result of our coaching sessions?
- What tangible changes would you see if this exceeded all your expectations?

A useful tool to facilitate this conversation is the values compass (see Chapter 22, What really matters). This has four different quadrants that ask about different domains, including work (meaningful activities, study), health (physical health, well-being, mental health, spiritual health), love (relationships, family, friends) and play (relaxation, fun, leisure). Using the compass, ask the coachee the degree to which they are living as the kind of person they want to be. A score of 10 represents them taking lots of actions towards the person they want to be and a 0 suggests there are limited actions towards who they want to be in that domain. On completion, the coachee can then be asked which of the domains they wish to strengthen and specifically, what valued actions in this area may look like.

Information gathering

In most coaching situations, it's important to be efficient and targeted when it comes to gathering information. This includes information of relevance to the key issue at hand, the historical development of the issue and goals related to the issue. Once goals for sessions have been spoken about, it's useful to draw out the information to make sense of how the coachee understands their situation, weaving this in with a structure that points to a functional understanding. The Matrix tool (see Chapter 14 for a fuller account of the Matrix in ACC) offers an excellent way to do this and leads to assessment questions such as:

- What is it that gets in the way of you moving towards your goals?
- What are the internal barriers?
- What are the external barriers?
- When those barriers show up, how do you typically respond?
- What's important to you about making this change?
- Broadly, who or what is important in life?
- When you have your values compass out and it's guiding your actions (and not the barriers), what kinds of actions would I be likely to see?

The answers to these questions will inform an understanding of the coachee's goals, and also where the coaching work will focus.

It is important to discuss the issue of workability of the coachee's strategies for change so far to help distinguish between those that have utility and those that, although they produce short-term outcomes, are not viable when considered in the context of values-based actions. In Chapter 16 we unpack this issue more fully.

Alongside these questions, it's useful to consider where the coachee's strengths and deficits lie related to the key skills of *Open, Aware* and *Active* (Oliver, Hill, & Morris, 2015). The *Open* domain refers to their ability to respond effectively to thoughts and emotions so that they no longer act as barriers to valued action. This is represented by skills on the left side of the Matrix. In the *Open* domain, what thoughts and feelings show up as the coachee moves towards what is important to them? How do they typically respond? Does the coachee fight and struggle with them? Do they passively give in to them?

Aware is being in the present moment in a way that is conscious, curious and flexible (the central component of the Matrix). In the *Aware* domain, it is good to determine the degree to which the coachee runs on autopilot, wrapped up in his or her own thoughts, about the past or future, particularly when it comes to taking steps in valued directions.

Active refers to the development of clarity on what matters most in life, and then pursuing those things vigorously. In the *Active* domain, look out for the degree to which coachees are able to articulate their values or whether they don't have a clear sense of what is important to them, giving answers simply to please you or saying what they think they should say.

Reference

Oliver, J., Hill, J., & Morris, E. (2015). *ACTivate Your Life: Using Acceptance and Mindfulness to Build a Life that Is Rich, Fulfilling and Fun*. London: Constable & Robinson.

14

The Matrix

The ACT Matrix (Polk, Schoendorff, Webster, & Olaz, 2016) is a powerful and efficient tool to bring together the key components of the model in a way that allows for a rapid functional analysis of behaviour in the context of values. It is particularly useful in a coaching context where efficient communication of the fundamentals of the model is important. It also allows coachees to increase awareness and make sense of their own responses and build increasingly larger patterns of committed action. It has applicability across a wide range of areas and is useful for coaching coachees who are both stuck and also those looking to maximise their performance.

The fact that it is a visual tool aids understanding and, in our experience, helps coachees engage with the material quickly (see Figure 14.1). It allows experiences to be functionally categorised and patterns to be identified more quickly.

The Matrix broadly sorts behaviour into two categories – that which is towards values (appetitive) and that which is a move away from values and governed by difficult or unwanted thoughts and feelings. In Figure 14.1, the horizontal line represents moves towards values (to the right) and moves away (to the left). The vertical line adds a second dimension, loosely categorised as internal experiences and external experiences and behaviour. The Matrix thus presents four quadrants which can be used to categorise thoughts, feelings, emotions and behaviour.

The right side of the Matrix refers to the active moves towards what is important. The bottom right quadrant talks to coachee's values and a useful metaphor to use here is that this quadrant is

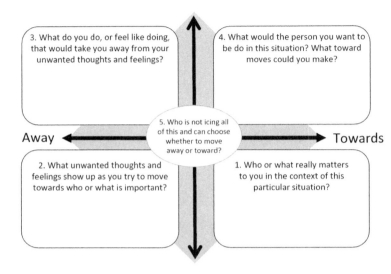

Figure 14.1 The Matrix (adapted by Richard Bennett)

like a compass that can be used as a guide to behaviour (see Chapter 10 for this metaphor). The top right quadrant refers to behaviours and actions taken when values are guiding us.

Of course, it's never so simple to just identify our values and the associated behaviours connected with these. It's a good place to start, but in normal circumstances, thoughts, feelings, memories and physical sensations show up in response to values-based action. These may include feelings like fear, tension, sadness and anger. Thoughts such as "What if I fail?", "I don't have what it takes!", "I'm not the kind of person that does this kind of thing". It is the bottom left quadrant of the Matrix that captures these.

The final quadrant, top left, refers to all the behaviours we do when the content from the bottom left quadrant arrives *and* we are caught up by it. In this place, we work hard to untangle ourselves from this content, reduce it or make it go away. When this happens, it can be said that behaviour comes under *aversive control*. The possibility of values guiding behaviour reduces dramatically, and any action is largely governed by whatever content shows up and responses to it.

In using the Matrix, it's helpful to go through the diagram with a coachee, written out on a piece of paper and explain the key principles of towards and away, and what each of the quadrants refers to. However, to really bring it alive, it's important to go through an actual example the coachee is experiencing in their own lives. There is no fixed place to begin, but normally a helpful place to start is the bottom right, asking within a specific situation, "Who or what is important to you?". The natural next place to move to is bottom left, asking, "What thoughts or feelings show up that could act as barriers to you expressing your values?". Next is to move to the top left, and ask, "When those internal barriers show up, and they've caught you, what do you do to move away from them?". Then, draw attention to the last quadrant, top right, and ask, "And what action(s) would you take, if you were choosing, based on what or who is important to you?". Finally, bring the coachee's attention to the circle in the middle of the Matrix and ask, "Who is noticing all of this and who gets to choose?". This question emphasises the observing, self-as-contact perspective that is brought into this exercise.

These questions begin to help the coachee disentangle their experience and their responses. They start to see these in relation to values and values-based action. Polk et al. (2016) refer to this activity as practising *Verbal Akido*, which is a great metaphor that captures the increased awareness and flexibility that coachees develop as they become proficient at the Matrix.

Along with developing the ability to categorise behaviour, it is important to draw out links between the different quadrants. The first link to make is between the bottom left and the top left quadrants. This helps highlight the association between thoughts and feelings and subsequent behaviours. For example, when a coachee is anxious and they engage in procrastination behaviours, then the behaviour is connected to the emotion. In addition, it is useful to draw out the ways in which such behaviours can function to exacerbate thoughts and feelings. For example, suppressing thoughts can lead to a rebound effect or avoiding emotions can increase their subsequent prominence. This helps to demonstrate to the coachee the ways in which loops or maintenance cycles can form.

A second important link to make is that between the bottom two quadrants. It's common for coachees to talk about values and unwanted thoughts and feelings as if they exist in opposition to each other. It's as if one precludes the other. It can be useful to illuminate the ways in which these are in fact two sides of the same coin. It's rare to take a genuine values-based move without a pang of anxiety or fleeting worries about failure. These are completely normal and often just the mind doing its best to look after and protect us. Awareness of this facilitates reductions in struggle with content, and can lead to a new appreciation of this content. Coachees say things such as "Ah, I'm feeling tense – that must mean I'm about to do something important!" or "The 'I'm at my limits' story just kicked in – I'm really exploring some new territory".

This leads to the last connection between the quadrants. If focusing on values naturally leads to an increased prominence of unwanted thoughts and feelings, then perhaps these could be used as prompts to undertake values-based action. This works as an alternative to the automatic pilot responses that are described in the top left of the quadrant. A prompt to link these quadrants could be, "When these thoughts and feelings show up (bottom left), what actions would you choose to take if you were in the driver's seat and acting as your best self?" (top right).

In this way, you can see how the Matrix moves the coachee right around the whole of the hexaflex. The left side quadrants emphasise the need for defusion and acceptance skills (*Open*).

The right side highlights values and committed action skills (*Active*). The middle suggests *Aware* skills, within which the coachee, along with the coach, adopts a new perspective within which behaviours are viewed in a functional context. This perspective-taking shift facilitates flexibility in the presence of unwanted thoughts and feelings so that the coachee can choose more effective action.

Reference

Polk, K. L., Schoendorff, B., Webster, M., & Olaz, F. O. (2016). *The Essential Guide to the ACT Matrix: A Step-by-Step Approach to Using the ACT Matrix Model in Clinical Practice*. Oakland, CA: New Harbinger Publications.

15

Formulation

At the heart of any effective ACT coaching session is a live, working functional formulation of the main issues the coachee is presenting – be it stuckness or wanting to maximise performance. The formulation is the shared map for the work and helps coach and coachee understand, collaborate and plan together.

A good formulation will help the coachee make sense of the situation they find themselves in order to develop a shared language. This is where the "engine" of the problem is identified, so it becomes clear what drives the problem and keeps it going. The information gathered from the assessment session (see Chapter 13) is used to provide the roadmap for the formulation.

By using the Matrix (see Chapter 14) this information can then be usefully presented to the coachee to highlight the impact of the behaviour when hooked by unwanted thoughts or feelings. This is then contrasted with behaviour guided by values. This allows the coachee to better discriminate the functions of their behaviour, particularly in terms of short-terms gains (for example, avoidance of a difficult task and the accompanying unwanted experiences) and long-term costs (for example, not achieving important goals as a result of procrastination).

Central to any good formulation work is the identification of cycles or behaviour the coachee engages in that keeps them stuck. For example, they may wish to address a lack of confidence when interacting with senior colleagues. In making sense of this ACC looks to break down the coachee's response when thoughts and feelings of low confidence appear. If, for example, a coachee typically responds by going into his or her shell in the presence of senior colleagues, a coach may wish to unpack the short- (feeling less anxious or safer) and long-term consequences (not pushing or challenging themselves in difficult situations).

Using the matrix, this can then be visually presented back to the coachee in order to demonstrate the ways in which a very understandable and natural response has unintended consequences. It is by identifying such unintended consequences that together the coach and coachee can start to unpick the ways in which certain behavioural responses may be less helpful. One of the advantages of using the Matrix as a framework is that it reduces the possibility that the coachee feels judged or criticised, as the behaviour is not evaluated as wrong but simply by whether it is helpful in terms of moving them towards their values.

Along with the stuck cycle, there is a corresponding virtuous cycle (see Figure 15.1) that seeks to identify alternative, more effective behavioural patterns. This emphasises defusion, acceptance and mindfulness as key skills to use in the context of an unwanted emotional response. This creates a new context within which this experience can be recognised as simply one part of the person, in addition to all the other parts of experience that exist in a continual state of flux. From this place of *self as context*, the possibility of choice based on values becomes a more prominent option. This increases the probability of towards moves and subsequent life expansion. The final part of the model refers to the coachee's learning history. This section highlights the ways in which they learned both helpful and unhelpful patterns of responding. For example, for a coachee who has a long history of procrastinating, it may be useful to know that they have a self-story of "I'm a failure" as a result of bullying, which rears its head any time the coachee approaches an important task. Conversely, for example, it's often useful to know if a coachee has a dealt with adversity and learned acceptance skills. Coaches don't typically spend a

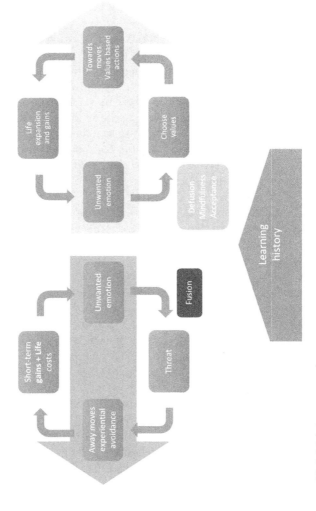

Figure 15.1 Maintenance cycles

Table 15.1 Formulation worksheet

Setting the scene
What are the coachee's goals for coaching?

Formulation
What is the key stuck issue the coachee is facing? What are the main processes that keep the person locked in stuckness? • What thoughts or self-stories is the coachee hooked on? • What emotions, sensations or memories are they avoiding? • How does fusion support experiential avoidance (e.g. "I can't handle this", "It's overwhelming", "It says something about me or my relationship to others") • What pulls them out of the present?
What are the payoffs for *away* moves? Do these contribute to a lack of progress?

What do *towards* moves look like? What values underpin *towards* moves? Who or what is important to them?

How does the coachee's history influence current responding?

Plan

Given these processes, what are the techniques and strategies that help unlock stuckness? What have you already tried?

Anything extra, in terms of knowledge and skills that you need to help you move forward with this plan?

great deal of time diving into the past, as compared to psychotherapy, as it's outside of the coaching remit. But a "light touch" on these issues can often be helpful.

An alternative method to highlight the different processes from the excellent book, *Mindful and Effective Employees* (Flaxman, Bond, & Livheim, 2013) is to use the "two sheets of paper" exercise (also known as the Flaxman manoeuvre). Here, the coach holds up two sheets of paper, on one written "Unwanted thoughts and feelings" and on the other "Values". The coach then holds up the first piece of paper (with "unwanted thoughts and feelings" written on it) so that it is closer the the coachee, with the second piece of paper sitting behind. This is used to describe the automatic pilot style within which unwanted thoughts and feelings guide behaviour. The coach then swaps the position of the pieces of paper so the second piece is closer to the coachee, indicating that the aim of the coaching work is to learn skills in order to do this so that the values become the more prominent guide to behaviour.

To help bring together all relevant information into a useful roadmap that assists formulation we've put together the worksheet in Table 15.1. After completing your assessment session we suggest filling in this worksheet to help develop a clear sense of the key issues for the coachee and how you might move forward.

Reference

Flaxman, P. E., Bond, F. W., & Livheim, F. (2013). *The Mindful and Effective Employee: A Training Program for Maximizing Employee Well-being and Effectiveness Using Acceptance and Commitment Therapy*. Oakland, CA: New Harbinger Publications.

16

The workability game

When initially laying out the ACC worldview in Chapter 1 (The world according to ACC), we said that central to the ACC philosophy is challenging a fundamental belief about the nature of "happiness". Namely that happiness is a state where pleasant thoughts and feelings outnumber unpleasant thoughts and feelings.

It is this widespread belief that lends itself to what is referred to to as the "control agenda" – the idea that if one can successfully control one's thoughts and feelings, then happiness, success, increased effectiveness and fulfilment will follow. In ACC we propose that, on the contrary, it is the continual struggle to control one's inner world that keeps people stuck and unfulfilled, that this is an unworkable strategy, and that acceptance and mindfulness are an effective alternative.

Given that this belief is so widely held and so strongly endorsed by our culture, an important early part of ACC with many coachees is consciously confronting this control agenda in a process that we call "the workability game" (it is usually referred to as "creative hopelessness" in the ACT world, but we find this to be a better fit with coaching work).

The intention of the workability game is to encourage the coachee to determine the *workability* of attempting to achieve positive change by trying to avoid or control thoughts and feelings i.e. do these strategies help them move in the direction of their values?

The aim is not to persuade or convince the coachee of the unworkability of the control agenda. Usually the workability game takes the form of a conversation where the coach invites the coachee to reflect on their use of "control strategies" in the past. A control strategy is any behaviour which has the principal aim of avoiding or getting rid of unpleasant private experiences, such as distraction, procrastination, rationalising and self-talk.

Of course, many people would say that they successfully use self-talk in certain situations, and that it helps them to be more effective. As ACC coaches our aim is not to suggest that all control strategies are bad and that our coachees should abandon them forthwith. Rather, we should be engaging them in a conversation about whether their habitual control strategies have shown themselves to be workable in the long term. If they have certain control strategies that seem to work then great. Most commonly coachees realise that the things they have been relying on to control their inner worlds in the past have been the very things that have been keeping them stuck.

In practice, a workability game conversation essentially involves asking these four questions:

1. What do you want from coaching?
2. What has got in the way of you achieving this is in the past?
3. What have you tried to manage this?
4. How has it worked, in the short term and the long term?

The first question – "What do you want from coaching?" – may well have already been covered during initial assessment, but it warrants revisiting as it leads neatly into the second and third questions, which are intended to identify control strategies.

The second question – "What has got in the way of you achieving this in the past?" – has the potential to direct coachees to factors external to them, so it's possible that as a coach you may need to do some work to orientate them back towards how they responded internally to these external factors. The aim is to identify the internal experiences that they see as having blocked them.

The third question – "What have you tried to manage this?" – is where we are specifically looking for control strategies. Given that our coachees tend not to think of their behaviours as "control strategies", the coach may need to do a certain amount of prompting. A helpful exercise to do here is known as "Join the D.O.T.S" (Harris, 2009). "D.O.T.S" is an acronym for four major types of control strategy.

Distraction (things designed to distract from thoughts and feelings like watching TV, games, phone, other tasks etc.)

Opting out (anything that involves avoidance, procrastination or withdrawal)

Thinking strategies (anything that involves trying to think your way out of it – worrying, fantasising, positive thinking, problem-solving, planning, self-criticism, analysing, debating, denial, beating yourself up etc.)

Substances (anything that involves putting any substance into the body, including food, cigarettes or alcohol, as well as prescription or illicit drugs)

The aim of Join the D.O.T.S is to help coachees to make the functional link between what might seem like unrelated behaviours, and notice their reliance on control strategies.

The fourth question – "How has it worked?" – is where we invite the coachee to assess the consequences of control, both short- and long-term. Both of these perspectives are important, and there are doubtless short-term benefits to control strategies – usually the temporary cessation of uncomfortable thoughts and feelings. However, an honest assessment of the long-term costs usually reveals that attempts to avoid or push away unwanted internal experiences mean missing out on opportunities, a disconnect from values, a life that gets smaller, and important goals remaining perpetually out of reach.

With most coachees, a short conversation framed around these four questions should be sufficient. A coachee who acknowledges that past reliance on control strategies has been ineffective may only need to be invited by the coach to partner with them in trying something new. There may be others who struggle to let go of the control agenda. These may be high-achievers who pride themselves on their capacity for self-control, and see it as having been important to their success in the past. Or it may simply be people who have relied on control strategies for a long time, and worry about what it would mean to give them up.

This needn't be an obstacle to coaching. In fact, it will be useful information so you can make a conscious choice about where to start. Focusing on values early on may be helpful, as it will go some way to giving the coachee a sense of why it might be worth considering loosening their attachment to control. The clearer their sense of their values, the clearer they can be on whether their control strategies are indeed taking them closer to or further from those values, and the clearer they can be on what there is to gain from experimenting with new strategies. Some early work on acceptance may be helpful, as it will help the coachee feel more equipped to manage any uncomfortable feelings that arise as they consider letting go of some of those control strategies. Alternatively, some mindfulness and self-as-context work could be helpful to help the coachee get a little bit of distance from any self-stories that might be supporting the control agenda (perhaps stories about being independent, self-sufficient or "strong").

Reference

Harris, R. (2009). *ACT Made Simple: An Easy to Read Primer on Acceptance and Commitment Therapy*. Oakland, CA: New Harbinger Publications.

17

Use of metaphor

In Chapter 3 (Relational Frame Theory for dummies) we described how the learned capacity to symbolically relate objects, concepts and ideas to each other using different "frames", while a very handy ability, was also at the heart of the psychological inflexibility that keeps so many of us and our coachees stuck. The good news is that, as coaches, we have a wonderful tool that exploits the very same mechanism to help get our coachees unstuck and moving towards their values. That tool is the metaphor.

There is a long history of metaphors being used in counselling, therapy and coaching. They are a great way of facilitating new perspectives, and making potentially complex ideas simple and memorable. Often coachees will spontaneously come up with metaphors during a session to convey something hidden or hard to explain, and these can be a great jumping off point for powerful coaching conversations. However, the types of metaphors that we consciously seek to employ in ACC are functional rather than just descriptive. As coaches we consciously use them to evoke behavioural change by providing coachees with new relational frames that facilitate new perspectives on their experience. In doing so, different options for action become available.

The aim is to transfer the functions within the relational network in the metaphor (the "vehicle") to the coachee's relational network (the "target"). Let's use the example of the "beach ball" metaphor. The aim of this is to illustrate the futility and the life-draining impact of trying to suppress thoughts and feelings we don't like. We compare the attempt to do so as like going to the seaside and trying to hold a beach ball under water. It can be done, but while you're holding it down there you can't get involved with the fun, splashy, seaside games. Plus it's tiring, and as soon as you let your guard drop, up it pops again. Here the function of trying to hold the beach ball under water is transferred to the attempt to suppress uncomfortable thoughts and feelings through a relational frame of coordination. If the coachee can connect with this, a shift becomes possible. More than likely they did not previously see the relationship between their suppression of thoughts and feelings and their stuckness. Not only that, now an alternative way of responding is implicitly suggested: to simply let the beach ball float there as they have fun in the water, or to allow the thoughts and feelings to be there as they actively engage with their values.

Using these principles an ACC coach can create their own metaphors to suit individual coachees and their specific pre-senting problems. And there is also huge range of wonderful metaphors already out there in the public domain. Whether coming up with a brand new metaphor, or using one of ACC's "classics" there are a few things to consider:

- Is there a match between the functions described in the metaphor and the functional relationships of the issue the coachee is facing? (If you are working with someone who reports their main issue as being a struggle to maintain focus in important meetings, the beach ball metaphor might not be the most appropriate or helpful one).

- Is the purpose of the metaphor clear? (In the beach ball metaphor, the details about friends having fun in the surf whilst the coachee stands with their hands under water makes it clear that the purpose is to encourage them to disengage from struggle *and also* use that as a platform to do more of what matters).

- Does the metaphor link to the coachee's own sphere of experience? (At best, as you get to know your coachee you will get a sense of their personal interests and frames of reference, and can create metaphors that make use of these.

At the very least, if you are using an established metaphor, be sure that it is something the coachee has understanding of, or can relate to).

As we said, there are countless wonderful metaphors already available for you to incorporate into your coaching. *The Big Book of ACT Metaphors* (Stoddard & Afari, 2014) is an invaluable resource here, full of great examples and comprehensive instructions. Below are a few of our favourite and most used metaphors (not referenced elsewhere in this book!):

Thought and defusion metaphors

- *The mind as a problem-solving machine*: The idea of the mind as a machine that is constantly looking for problems to solve – sometimes this is helpful, but some things (difficult thoughts and emotions for instance) are not necessarily "problems" and cannot be "solved".
- *Thoughts as tools*: Similar to the above. Just as every tool in a toolbox has a specific use, thoughts are great for some things (strategising, planning), and less good for others (learning to play an instrument, having a heartfelt conversation).

Emotions and acceptance metaphors

- *The unwelcome party guest*: If an unwelcome guest crashes your party you can spend all your time trying to get rid of him, but you will miss the party. In the same way, trying to constantly manage uncomfortable feelings can disengage you from your life and the world around you.

Values metaphors

- *The light on the hill*: Our values are like a light at the top of a hill, guiding us from afar as we navigate through life.

- *Tending a garden*: Acting on values is like tending a garden – you need to prepare the ground, sow the seeds and then wait. It may take a bit of time to see the evidence, but with regular tending the green shoots will begin to show.

Self as context and observing self metaphors

- *Life as a stage show*: Life is like a stage show, and on the stage are all of our thoughts, feelings, memories, sensations. The observing self is that part of us that can sit back and just watch as the action plays out on stage.

Workability metaphors

- *Polygraph test*: Try as we might, we cannot "control" or switch off our emotions. If hooked up to a polygraph machine and told at gun-point not to feel anxious, most of us would fail.

Reference

Stoddard, J. A., & Afari, N. (2014). *The Big Book of ACT Metaphors: A Practitioner's Guide to Experiential Exercises and Metaphors in Acceptance and Commitment Therapy*. Oakland, CA: New Harbinger Publications.

18

Facilitating cognitive defusion

Cognitive defusion is the process of moving into that metaphorical space between us and our thoughts, the place from which we can engage consciously and respond intentionally to our thought content, with flexibility and non-judgement.

Given that we as humans do have a tendency to associate closely with the "mind", a bit of psychoeducation can be helpful when introducing defusion. A metaphor that we like to introduce here is of the mind as a sophisticated "don't get killed machine". We present a mini-history of the evolution of the mind, which functioned in early man only to keep him alive, constantly looking out for potential threats to life and limb. Now, 100,000 years on, we may not encounter the same mortal threats day by day, but the mind is still on the look-out for potential threats – failure, embarrassment, losing a job and a thousand and one other things. So the brain evolved to keep us safe from negative experiences. And that is really helpful some of the time! But other times it can keep us trapped in our comfort zone, away from doing stuff that might be important or rewarding.

A couple of things are worth specifically pointing to in the example above. First is that we can continually reinforce defusion simply through the language that we use. By referring to "the mind" as a distinct entity in itself we encourage the coachee to acknowledge the distinction between them and their thought content. We can do this throughout the session:

"What is your mind telling you right now?"
"Sounds like your mind was really giving you a hard time."

"So you wanted to go and speak to him, but your mind kind of got in the way?"

Another metaphor that can be used to amplify this is that of the mind as a "master storyteller". The metaphor here is that the mind is constantly scanning the world outside and inside of us to understand what is happening and why. It doesn't like gaps or inconsistencies – it likes things to add up or make sense. Unfortunately, the world doesn't always give us complete information, so where there is a gap in our understanding, we create a "story" to fill that gap. For example, let's imagine that a team leader in a company is giving a briefing to her direct reports when she notices one of them yawn. In that moment – perhaps because of previous experiences or beliefs – she sees that yawn and her mind throws up the "boring story": *"She's yawning ... people yawn when they are bored ... I'm talking ... I must be boring"*.

Most people can relate to this experience, and we can use this "storytelling" concept as a great way of facilitating defusion. For instance, one popular exercise involves asking a coachee to speak out loud all of the thoughts that their mind throws at them when they are in a challenging situation, exactly as they sound in their head. The coach writes these verbatim on a piece of paper or card. They then repeat these back to the coachee and ask them to imagine that they are lines of dialogue in a story. The coach then asks "What name would you give to that story"? They then write the name of the story on the other side of the card, in the context of a short sentence intended to lighten it, or mitigate its emotional impact (for example: "Hello, the I'm Boring Story"; or "Ah ha! It's the I'm Boring Story"). The coachee is invited to spend some time looking at the original thoughts as written, while consciously fusing with them – really buying into them, experiencing them as if they were true. She is then invited to flip the card over and notice how it feels when she sees the story reflected back to her in this particular way.

The thing to emphasise to the coachee here is that the thoughts have not gone anywhere; she is perfectly at liberty to flip the card back over and get right back into them. All that has changed is her relationship to the thoughts. Usually there is a feeling of just a little distance from them, more of a sense of choice about how to respond. This is one of the essential qualities we are going for with defusion work: a feeling of distance and choice, achieved through an experiential exercise that dares to approach what might be difficult or uncomfortable internal content with openness and curiosity. These can be as simple as encouraging the coachee to carry flash cards with questions written on them, designed to bring their thoughts into conscious awareness ("What is my mind saying right now?"; "What do I get from buying into this story?"; "If I were to choose, what action would I take?"). Or they can be as apparently wacky as inviting a coachee to literally "thank" her mind when an unhelpful or unworkable thought shows up (*Mind: "This is pointless, these people aren't taking you seriously"; Coachee: "Thanks Mind!"*).

Care must be taken when trying out exercises like these. The intention is to create defusion by changing the context in which these thoughts are experienced – from one of heaviness and literal truth, to one of lightness and choice. However, we'd propose always asking for permission to "try something out" when introducing such exercises, and to remain sensitive to the coachee's responses. Done insensitively or without such awareness, irreverence can seem like disrespect or lack of care.

What is great about exercises like those described above is that they can be energising, counterintuitive and even fun. They can create a whole different experience around thought content that might well have been blocking a coachee for many years, and promote a collaborative dynamic in the session.

However, this is not the only way to facilitate defusion. There are slower, more meditative exercises that are perfect for practising the art of simply noticing one's thinking. Often we are so caught up in the flow of the "thinking mind" that we do not even notice it, so the foundation of defusion is in simply noticing the process of thought as it unfolds.

Perhaps the most well known of the meditative defusion exercises is "Leaves On A Stream". Here the coachee is guided by the coach to imagine his consciousness as like a river, with leaves flowing by on the surface. Each time a thought arises he is invited to place that thought on a leaf and allow it to flow by in its own time. The coachee is encouraged not to rush thoughts away, but to simply place them on a leaf and let them flow away. The coach may hold them in this space, repeating the simple instructions to notice if they have been hooked by a thought and to place it on a leaf in their own time, for anywhere between 5 and 15 minutes. With practice, this helps to build the defusion muscle – the capacity to notice thoughts as they arise; to experience them not as truths or commands, but simply thoughts; and to allow them to come and go without judgement or attachment.

Again, as coach and coachee you can collaborate to make this exercise as personal and evocative as you want. Instead of leaves on a stream you may visualise thoughts as cars passing by a window, clouds moving across the sky, or whatever image seems to resonate most with your coachee.

These are just a small selection of literally hundreds of metaphors and exercises that can be employed during a coaching session. It is in doing this stuff, rather that talking about it, that it comes to life. And, as with every other part of the ACC process, it is vital to emphasise to coachees the importance of regular practice.

19

From struggle to acceptance

It pays to be mindful about how acceptance is introduced and delivered to a new coachee. This is partly because – as mentioned in Chapter 7 (Acceptance) – the term can sound passive or negative. In addition to this, the world of emotions is one where there may be unhelpful beliefs that have to be addressed for the coachee to fully engage with the process. We have already established that culturally the concept of "happiness" has become conflated with an absence of "negative" emotion. And while there is an increasing awareness of the importance of emotional and social intelligence in the workplace and beyond, there remain some commonly held cultural beliefs about the role of emotions and how best to work with them. It is still common to encounter those who believe that emotions should be "left at the door" and not brought into the workplace, that they necessarily get in the way of good decision-making or that "negative" emotions are toxic.

It is not uncommon to encounter coachees who insist that they are great at controlling their emotions, and that their capacity to do so has been central to their success thus far. With coachees who are doggedly attached to this perspective, a return to the "workability game" may be in order. Otherwise, consider simply positioning acceptance as a helpful alternative way of managing emotions, another "tool in the toolbox" to run alongside those they have acquired already, to give them more range and choice.

Given that this may or may not be something that our coachees are accustomed to reflecting on and talking about, early work might be focused on encouraging them to simply notice, register and label their emotions. This could be as between-session homework (with guidance from the kind of worksheet you might find in our 2015 self-help book *ACTivate Your Life* by Oliver, Hill, and Morris), or in-session.

Whether in or between sessions, the essence of acceptance work is to encourage coachees to notice their emotions, register them as sensations in the body and, rather than struggle with or try to change them, willingly come into contact with them. A classic exercise to facilitate this process is known as "physicalising". Here the coachees are guided through a process where they are invited to reflect on a situation that evokes some tricky or unpleasant emotion, and to locate that feeling in the body. They are then asked to focus their attention on it, and to imagine it as a physical object in as much detail as they can – its shape, its weight, its texture. In some versions the coachee is asked to imagine the object floating out of the body and hovering in front of them, so they can get an even better look. Finally – and crucially – they are asked to willingly take the object back into the body

When debriefing the coachee's experience of this exercise, they may report that in some way the feeling changed over the course of the exercise – that it shrank or reduced, or in some way they felt better. Here it is very important that the coach emphasise that if they experienced some change that is a pleasant bonus, but that it is not the aim of the exercise – the aim is simply to observe the emotion with curiosity and non-judgement. To imply that a change in the feeling is a "good" result is to play into the control agenda that we are trying to undermine.

Longer, more meditative, eyes-closed exercises like physicalising are great for really getting coachees to take a closer look at their emotions. Equally as powerful are the moments during the course of any session when emotion shows up, which we can use to experiment with willingness and acceptance. Again, while some of our coachees may be highly emotionally intelligent, others may have bought into cultural stories that encourage us to switch off to our feelings. As a coach, simply being alive to the moments when the coachee seems to be experiencing a heightened emotion is important. In these moments we can ask them: "What emotion just showed up?"; "Where do you feel it?". We can invite the coachee to just sit with the emotion and notice its presence. We can offer a simple instruction to "breathe into" or "make some space for" the feeling.

These are the moments where the coachee gets to notice emotion as it comes up, and to do something different from what comes naturally to most people – avoid or struggle with it. The "quicksand metaphor" perfectly captures the ACC approach to acceptance of emotions. When caught in quicksand, the most natural response would be to struggle, fight and try to pull oneself free. But it is this struggling that, in fact, makes us sink faster. The way to escape from quicksand is to – against all our better instincts – lie back and come into full contact with the surface of the sand. Only then do we rise to the top and have freedom to move once more.

As with every other part of the ACC model, it is important to keep a focus on values when working with acceptance. A question that is likely to be present, if not specifically articulated, is "Why"? "Why should I willingly come into contact with unpleasant or uncomfortable emotions?". The answer to that question is in our values. We propose that not only is it necessary to accept the presence of emotion in order to navigate effectively towards our values, but that emotions themselves are a helpful source of information about our values. Often a move towards an important value will involve some kind of behaviour that takes us out of our comfort zone. When we make these moves, emotion tends to show up. From this perspective uncomfortable emotions aren't something to be avoided, suppressed or disregarded. They are a sign that we are doing something that matters.

An exercise that makes this relationship between emotion and valued action tangible involves asking the coachee to write down on one side of a piece of paper something important that they want to do (for instance, delivering a training session to a senior management team). On the other side of the piece of paper ask the coachee to write the feelings that they find themselves struggling with when they consider this action (perhaps anxiety). Put it to them that we could throw the paper in the bin and get rid of that anxiety. But if we did so, it would mean throwing away the valued action as well – one necessarily accompanies the other. Indeed the presence of the discomfort is a sign that the coachee is doing something that they care about.

This exercise could also be used as an example of the inevitability of what we call "clean pain". By "clean pain" we mean the normal and natural uncomfortable emotions that are part of living a full life. If you are really living life and doing what matters this stuff will show up. "Dirty pain" happens when we respond to this normal and natural part of the human experience in a closed way – when we try to push this part of our experience away from us. We start giving ourselves a hard time for feeling a certain way, we compare ourselves to others who look like they're coping better and we end up working extra hard to block out the emotion. As a result, we end up feeling not only the original feeling, but a whole lot of extra "dirty" feelings on top of that – frustration, annoyance, guilt, shame, the list goes on. While all this is going on, we deprive ourselves of energy and the opportunity to do things that matter to us.

In a nutshell, working with coachees around acceptance is about supporting them in building the skills to stop generating "dirty pain" through struggle, and to willingly accept the "clean pain" that shows up as they take committed action in service of their values.

Reference

Oliver, J., Hill, J., & Morris, E. (2015). *ACTivate Your Life: Using Acceptance and Mindfulness to Build a Life that Is Rich, Fulfilling and Fun*. London: Constable & Robinson.

20

Be here now

Helping coachees to contact the present moment

The key skill that we are supporting the development of here is that of "mindfulness". It can be useful to describe to a new coachee what is meant by this term, as it is one that has now firmly entered the public consciousness and may be open to misunderstanding. In our book *ACTtivate Your Life*, we described mindfulness as *"being aware of the present moment, in a way that is conscious, curious, and flexible"* (Oliver, Hill, & Morris, 2015). What most coaches find is that, even if all coachees don't necessarily have a clear understanding of what mindfulness means from an ACC perspective, almost all can relate to the experience of being physically "here and now" but mentally "there and then". More and more coachees talk about how the demands of their perpetually busy lives make it hard for them to truly be "in the moment" and how they feel the impact on their effectiveness and well-being.

When introducing this part of the ACC model it may be helpful to emphasise this pragmatic intent – to tell the coachee that you will be doing some exercises and exploring some terrain that might feel unusual, but the intention is that coming into closer contact with the present moment is key to being more effective and more fulfilled. Steve Hayes, one of the originators of the ACT model, pretty much summed up the intention of this work the in the title of perhaps his most famous book: *Get Out of Your Mind and into Your Life* (Hayes & Smith, 2005). Contacting the present moment is a key to being more effective and fulfilled.

For most coachees, positioning mindfulness in this way should be enough to engender willingness to try it out. Others may also benefit from reassurance that, while certain exercises do have a meditative quality, it is not meditation per se, and there is no necessity of any religious or spiritual belief. And the great thing is that, while there are some classic longer eyes-closed exercises, there are others that can be done in the flow of day-to-day life, without needing to specifically make space or time.

The most common starting point for contacting the present moment is a mindful breathing exercise. Here the coach will guide the coachee in consciously focusing their awareness on the simple physical sensation of breathing. As a coach you will instruct them to simply notice the feeling of their stomach rising and falling, air passing in through the nose and mouth and so on, sometimes with a suggestion that they bring a quality of curiosity to that noticing (like a "curious scientist", or perhaps "like a space alien that has never observed breathing before"). Periodically invite the coachee to notice if they have drifted into thinking and, if so, to gently bring their awareness back to the present moment, using the breath as an "anchor".

Such an exercise might be as short as 5 minutes or as long as 10 minutes (probably no longer than this in a standard coaching session). Once the exercise has come to an end, take time to debrief with the coachee. This could be done using the "heart, head and hands" model we describe in Chapter 22 (What really matters):

> *Heart:* What did you notice as we went through that exercise?
> *Head:* How does this experience fit in with what we've spoken about so far in the session today, and in our coaching together?
> *Hands:* How do you think you could use some of these insights in your life out there in the real world?

There are a couple of common responses that we should be on the lookout for here (or with any mindfulness exercise). One is the coachee who says that they found the experience "relaxing" or something similar. If that is the case, it is vital that we as coaches respond in a neutral way, emphasising that while a feeling of relaxation is not unusual, it should be considered a "bonus", and is not the intention of the exercise. If we buy into the idea that achieving a state of relaxation (or a reduction in rate or intensity of unwanted thoughts or feelings) is a "positive" outcome of any mindfulness exercise, we are buying into the very control agenda that we are looking to help our coachees detach from.

An alternative response is that "it didn't work" or something similar – the coachee reports that their mind was busy and they were unable to properly focus on their breathing. Again, it is important that we do not affirm the idea that finding the exercise challenging is evidence of it "not working". To do so is to buy into the idea that the aim is to achieve stillness of mind and shut down thoughts. In fact, such a response is a great moment to emphasise that mindfulness is not a state to be achieved, but a skill to be developed. It is the act of noticing a mind that has been hooked unhelpfully, and consciously choosing to return awareness to the present moment that represents the process of mindfulness at work. Each time one does this, the "mindfulness muscle" is strengthened.

Reference to the metaphorical "mindfulness muscle" can be really helpful. For a start what it implies is that mindfulness is not a magical ability that some have and others don't, it is a capacity within all of us – it's just that most of us don't consciously access it that often, so it is not that strong. With a bit of work we can strengthen it. It also means that we can extend the metaphor when emphasising the importance of practice. If you want to strengthen a muscle at the gym you need to work it – one sit-up doesn't make a six-pack! Similarly, we need to encourage our coachees to practise, and support them in doing so. A realistic suggestion might be to propose that coachees practise mindful breathing for five minutes a day for the first week, perhaps increasing by two or three minutes every couple of days over the course of the second week. While this is an exercise that can be entirely self-directed, it can be helpful to supply coachees with a recording of your voice to guide them, initially at least. Alternatively, share a link to one of the many available audio recordings online (here is one created by us: https://contextualconsulting.co.uk/resources).

There are a host of mindfulness exercises that can be done in-session which follow the same essential structure as mindful breathing. Some involve the coachee consciously connecting with stimuli in the external environment (things they can see, hear, smell or feel). Others involve shining the spotlight of awareness inward to focus on thoughts and feelings – noticing them as they come and go in that mindful spirit of consciousness, curiosity and flexibility. It is here that we see the intersection of contacting the present moment with acceptance and defusion – each of these processes can only take place in the here and now.

The more the coachee is able to mindfully observe their thoughts and feelings, the more they can observe their own patterns and habits and get a sense of their mind at work; the more they can do this, and consciously anchor themselves in the present moment, the greater their capacity to take conscious, values-led action.

And we think is important to emphasise that contacting the present moment isn't just about being more effective – it is also about living fully and bringing richness to experience. A life on autopilot is a life half-lived. Many of our coachees have reported that, while they seem to be "doing all the right things", their sense of engagement with the process of living has suffered. What is wonderful is that there are a number of mindfulness exercises that explicitly aim to connect the coachee with this richness and fulfilment. Even better, many of these can be practised easily and practically in the flow of day-to-day life. We will explore this further in Chapter 25 (Mindfulness on the move).

References

Hayes, S. C., & Smith, S. (2005). *Get Out of Your Mind and into Your Life: The New Acceptance and Commitment Therapy.* Oakland, CA: New Harbinger Publications.

Oliver, J., Hill, J., & Morris, E. (2015). *ACTivate Your Life: Using Acceptance and Mindfulness to Build a Life that Is Rich, Fulfilling and Fun.* London: Constable & Robinson.

21

Introducing self as context

In coaching work a focus on the self might not always be explicit but it runs through everything we do. Whether the focus is on increasing performance, working through a stuck situation or developing a personal change programme, the issue of the person doing the work, is always there. What does it mean to make such changes? Who are you to be going be at the next level? What does the story you tell yourself about who you are, say about what you can and cannot do here?

In any work, and especially in coaching, it's crucial to make the topic of "the self" less mystical and much more concrete and practical. Here are some key steps to focus on.

Introduce the idea of self-stories in a practical and relevant way

It's important to choose language that works for the coachee and captures how we all develop a narrative about who we are, based on our past experiences. We've found that most coachees are fine with the term "story", but about 1 in 10 people will find the term invalidating as it sounds like something they've just made up and diminishes the truth of their experience. Here we would look for an alternative ("label", "the title on the book of you", or simply say, "the ways in which you describe yourself").

We aim to communicate to the coachee that self-stories are not good or bad, but sometimes, when they are held too rigidly, they can be problematic and stop us from responding flexibly. Most coachees will understand the issues with a "negative" self-story and limitations such as "I'm not intelligent" or "I'm a fraud". But they may not link how the same relationship with a "positive" self-story could equally lead to inflexibility. For example, "I'm a great coach" intuitively sounds very positive but, if held on to too tightly, could lead to inflexibility and resistance to new ideas or further training ("What's the point? I'm great already!"). With such examples we develop the idea that it's not merely the presence of the self-story that is the problem but more our relationship with it.

Conversations about self-stories need to be linked to valued actions, and are likely to be most relevant when the coachees are really stretching themselves and stepping outside their comfort zones. It is important to normalise this as a sign of a healthy mind at work, looking to protect the person by reminding them of their limitations and potential dangers and not as a fundamental truth

The next step is to help the coachee recognise the appearance of the self-story, what it is saying and how they are responding to it. In practice we call this "getting eyes on" the self-story. In introducing the concepts, we use the terms the "Thinking Self" and the "Observing Self":

Sometimes we talk about two different selves: the Thinking Self and the Observing Self. The Thinking Self evaluates, judges, criticises, problem-solves; all incredibly useful skills for your average human being. Of course, it likes to understand and make sense of things, including ourselves. As such, you may notice it pull together all of your memories, experiences, thoughts and feelings over the course of your life into a "simple" story about you. This has its benefits, for example, in helping you to understand yourself or predict how you might respond in certain situations or help you interact with others.

In contrast, the Observing Self is a perspective from which we get to watch and observe the Thinking Self in operation. It's the part of us that's not exactly thinking but the place from which

we can step back and observe all our thoughts feelings, sensations and memories. The Observing Self is like a torch in a dark room where a beam of light illuminates the objects of the Thinking Self.

Develop a metaphor that works for the coachee

A metaphor is a useful way to structure the coachee's experience and make discriminations between the Thinking Self and the Observing Self. Where possible it's useful to generate a metaphor with which the coachee has some personal experience so they are better able to relate to it. Having said that, a favourite of ours is the "Dancefloor and the Balcony" metaphor.

In life, a lot of the time we're on the dance floor, in the thick of it all. Moving to the music, responding to who or what is right in front of us and the track the DJ has cued up. This is like being wrapped up in our Thinking Self where our thoughts, feelings and self-stories largely govern our actions. And most of the time this works pretty well. But there is a different perspective to be had, from up on the balcony, watching yourself and others strutting about. This is the Observing Self. Notice how from this perspective you're not quite as involved in the action; there's more space, room to breathe and to take a broader perspective that may include other things aside from just what's on the dance floor at that moment. But notice how neither perspective is good or bad – each has its place. It just so happens that most of us spend a lot of our time in the thick of it on the dance floor, without spending much time on the balcony.

Build in practical exercises relevant to the coachee's main issues

There are three important skills to teach in relation to self-stories and helping to strengthen the perspective of the Observing Self. These we call the three Ns – Notice it, Name it and Now what?

Notice it

First of all, simply learn to notice the self-story in operation. What is it saying? What does it want? How are you responding to it? Is this helpful or unhelpful? It's useful to remind coachees about times when it's likely to be helpful to do a quick check in. Commonly, these times are when there is an opportunity to step out of comfort zones.

Name it

Once the self-story has been recognised, give it a name. This helps to more broadly catagorise the story and gather it together in a functional class ("Ah, there's my 'not good enough' story – it wants me to prevent me from taking a risk". Or "Right – I hear my 'unfair/not worth it' story".

This helps to engage the Observing Self, so as to defuse from the Thinking Self and the self-story that's shown up. Naming the self-story also helps the coachee to recognise the familiarity of it and the repetitiveness of it. Knowing that given a certain context (e.g. stepping outside of a comfort zone) it will reliably show up helps dial down the unpredictability and also the power a self-story has. From the perspective of the Observing Self, questions about chosen actions can legitimately occur.

Now what?

At this point it's helpful to bring in a values perspective with a question such as:

Given that you've noticed your self-story and you've named it, now what? What would a move that was based on your values look like right now?

This sequence is useful to practise multiple times in sessions and then set up ways to practice outside of meetings. We would commonly write "Notice", "Name" and "Now what?" on a card and ask coachee to pull it out several times a day and run through the questions. Or we'd suggest that they plug them into their phone reminder so they pop up at intervals during their week.

Link it to other key processes

As with any process, and especially so with self as context, it's important to link it together with other processes. With the three Ns method, values are built into the question "Now what?". In this way, the purpose of bringing self as context online is made explicit. Similarly, asking coachees to notice and name helps to promote a stance of mindful defusion from their self-stories as they connect with their Observing Self. Focusing on acceptance here will be useful in identifying points of struggle and suggesting a move towards openness.

22

What really matters

Success through values

Values work can be some of the most fun work in ACC, but it can also be the trickiest. Notice what shows up as you answer the following question:

What's important to you in life?

It's tough right? To answer the question, you need to be prepared to dive on into yourself and reach a conclusion that's genuine and honest. When doing values work, it's therefore very important to keep all other processes in mind, helping coachees to be mindfully open to emotions as they occur and aware of the variety of thoughts that might pop up. Good values work in coaching then looks at exploring and uncovering the coachee's values, attending to the emotional qualities of valuing, and setting a context within which valued actions can be taken. We talk about this as the *Head*, the *Hands* and the *Heart* of values work.

Head

Of course there are many ways to draw out values and help people to explore what matters to them. This is important work as it helps the coachee construct alternative sources of motivation, rather than whatever thoughts and feelings happen to be about at any particular moment. Just as setting a sail on a yacht collects energy from the wind, constructing values allows the coachee to "collect energy" as they move towards their values.

Curious questioning from a coach can go a long way to helping coachees contact their values:

- Who or what is important to you in life?
- If you could take action and no one would see, judge or hear about it, what would you do?
- If your actions didn't get any type of reward or praise, what would you choose to do?
- Tell me about a time in life when you were engaged, vital or alive. What were you doing? What made that experience important to you?

A useful tool to facilitate this conversation is the values compass. This asks coachees to rate themselves between 1 and 10 as to the degree to which they are living a life true to their values in four different life domains – work, health, love and play. On completion, the coachee can then be asked which of the domains they may wish to strengthen and specifically, what valued actions in this area may look like.

Conversations about *peak experiences* can be helpful ways to draw out values. The coachee is asked about a moment in life when they felt alive, vital and engaged. These points in life often speak to what is meaningful or purposeful for the coachee. The coach carefully asks questions about this moment, looking to illuminate and uncover values:

- What does that experience say about what matters to you?
- What direction would you be heading in so more peak moments are likely?
- What choices and actions need to happen to move you in that direction?

Finally, using tools such as values cards (available from www. contextualconsulting.co.uk) can be a creative way to explore values. Cards offer up a range of potential values that the coachee is asked to sort through, picking out ones that are relevant to them. Values described are varied and could include verbs such as "striving", "creating" or "connecting". After the coachee has selected some that are personally relevant, the coach can ask about times when the coachee has enacted on these in the past. Or ask about how actions in the future could be informed by these values.

Hands

Intertwined with values conversations is the call to action. This is covered more extensively in Chapter 23, but it's important to emphasise several key points when it comes to actually setting a context for values. Because of the nature of valuing, it's extra-ordinarily easy for both coachee and coach to spend lots of time *talking* about values in an abstract way and little time actually *doing* values. The doing of values includes setting tasks to take place outside of sessions to experiment with values.

But also, it's important to note that valuing can take place within a session. Sometimes, articulating a value is a valued action in and of itself. A values-savvy coach will be quick to pick up on this and draw the coachee's attention to this ongoing process of valuing as it's occurring live.

There are three qualities to the doing of values that are important:

1. *Experiment.* Encourage the coachee to try out new behaviours and really step outside of their comfort zone. This then has the feel of a practice ground, where the coachee gets to shake things up in interesting new combinations, and like a good scientist, gather new data on whether this kind of valuing works.
2. *Curiosity.* The coach can help the coachee to be mindfully curious about the results of values experiments, including the range of experiences and emotions that actually occurred

while undertaking values. This can help the coachee develop a better *felt* sense of valuing. So for example, anxiety that arises in the context of taking a valued action can then be learned to be appreciated rather than ignored.

3. *Right and wrongs.* It can be very easy for a coachee to beat themselves over the head with their values. By this we mean they judge themselves as have not having done those values perfectly. This is a situation that we probably want to avoid and it can be useful to remind coachees to hold their values *lightly*. This could include asking a coachee if it would be possible to be encouraging and respectful towards themselves at those points when they inevitably are not able to act on their values.

Heart

Values work invariably evokes emotion, sometimes in quite a strong way. It's therefore good to consider what represents the "Goldilocks" zone for your coachee. Too cool could mean it's all a little abstract and intellectual. Too hot and the client is likely to run a mile. Just right and the coach can bring the coachee into an optimum zone where they are challenged but not over extended.

In ACC, it is important that thoughts and emotions that arise from values work are normalised as part of the process. When not viewed as the enemy, we can ask our clients to be curious about them and what they may say about what's important. In this way, the functions of these experiences are transformed from something threatening to an indicator of valued action. Rather than "Stop!", it can be read as "Valuing taking place! Push on!".

23

Helping coachees take committed action

While goal-setting and action planning will be processes familiar to any coach, the ACC coach will approach them slightly differently to those working with other models.

The role of the ACC coach when it comes to committed action includes the following:

- Helping coachees to create values-based goals, or to link pre-existing goals to values
- Helping coachees to break down goals, and create workable action plans
- Using setbacks as an opportunity to *continually develop psychological flexibility*

It is this last point in particular that distinguishes the work of the ACC coach from those using other models or approaches. But let's address each point in turn.

Linking goals and values

An important role of an ACC coach is to help coachees make the distinction between goals and values, and impress upon them the importance of the two being complementary. In a society (particular the culture of business and work) where goal-achievement is often regarded as the only metric of success, it is very common to come across individuals who have spent a lifetime striving towards goals that are not necessarily consistent with their values. What these people tend find is that, on achievement of these goals, the anticipated feeling of fulfilment fails to materialise. However, the cultural story of "success = happiness" is so deeply ingrained that the automatic pilot response is often to conclude that what is needed is more "success". So the individual sets more (possibly values-inconsistent) goals, charges towards these, experiences the same outcome, and the process begins again.

We owe it to our coachees to put it to them (if necessary) that:

a) Goals that are consistent with your values are more likely to be achieved than those that are not. At some point you will hit an obstacle that will leave you asking: "Why am I doing this? What is the purpose of this action?". If you have a clear answer to this question you are more likely to persist, and to bring more energy and engagement to whatever it is you are doing.

b) Our energy is best invested in goals that are consistent with our values, rather than those that aren't. These are the ones that are most likely to bring us fulfilment.

In practice, we would suggest that values clarification takes place before formally entering into the process of goal-setting and action planning. When the time comes for a conversation around goals and objectives, the ACC coach should be willing to challenge the client to make a clear link between the goal and their values, to amend their goals to make them more values-consistent, or even to create entirely new values-consistent goals. As coach and counselor Richard Blonna (2011) says "You might be the first person to look the client in the eye and say 'So how do these values relate to what's important to you as a person?'".

Breaking down goals and creating an action plan

As well as helping coachees to form goals that are values based, the ACC coach can also be of service by helping coachees to create workable goals and a clear action plan to achieve them.

One feature of a workable goal is that it is something that can be *actively* strived towards and engaged with. On this note, we warn coachees against "dead person's goals". These can be described as anything that a dead person can do more effectively that a live human being. "Stop talking over people in meetings" is a dead person's goal. "Stop working on weekends" is something that a corpse could do better than a live human being. Help your coachees construct goals based on what it is that they *want to do*, rather than what they *don't want to do* or want to do less of.

Helpfully, a common frame of reference for most coaches and coaching coachees will be the concept of SMART goals. Just as many people use the SMART principle when creating objectives in the workplace, it is worth encouraging coachees to bring the same level of rigour and clarity to their own personal goal-setting. Once long- to medium-term values-based goals are set, we can help our coachees to create clear actions that will help them move towards them. Harris (2009) suggests a slightly different interpretation of SMART:

Specific: It needs to be absolutely clear exactly want the client intends to do, and how. "Spend more social time with work colleagues" is an intention. "Invite three work colleagues to lunch this week" is a specific action.

Meaningful: Is this action something that has personal meaning? Is it clear how this not only takes you a step closer to your goal, but that it is a conscious step in the direction of your values?

Adaptive: Does this action represent a step that is likely to enrich your life? By pursuing this action are you building your psychological flexibility?

Realistic: It's great to be ambitious, but unrealistic goals are risky. While it's inevitable that coachees will sometimes struggle or come up short, consistent failure to meet goals will only reinforce unhelpful thoughts and self-stories. Consistent successful action will create new associations that make future action easier and more likely.

Time-bound: By insisting on specificity, coach and client know what they intend to do and how. Being clear on when they will do it adds momentum and accountability, making positive action much more likely.

Using setbacks to reinforce psychological flexibility

Like any coach, one of the primary roles the ACC coach plays is to hold their client to account – to challenge them to do what they say they are going to do, and then check in with them as to whether they did it. And every coach will approach "failure" to follow through on action as an opportunity for the client to learn about what got in the way, and how they might approach things differently in the future.

However, the role of the ACC coach in supporting coachees around setbacks is a little different. From an ACC perspective, setbacks are not just inevitable, they are great! If the goals and actions that they have set for themselves are truly values based and SMART, it is almost inevitable that at some point a client will experience some internal obstacles – thoughts, feelings, sensations, memories, impulses that seem to be getting in the way of them taking action. As an ACC coach we welcome these as opportunities to practise using defusion, acceptance, willingness and contact with the present moment, to continue to build the skill of psychological flexibility and act on what matters even in the presence of unwanted internal experiences.

It's advisable to support a client in anticipating the potential internal obstacles she is likely to encounter as she pursues a particular action, and in setting an intention about how she will manage it if and when it shows up. These kinds of setbacks are also great to work with in-session – they can be the content for practical exercises building on the other core ACC processes.

A metaphor that we can introduce here involves asking the client to fold their arms "the other way" (i.e. left arm over right if they normally fold the right arm over the left, or vice versa). Ask the client how it feels to do this. Invariably they will say "weird" or "strange" or "uncomfortable". The learning point here is that whenever we adopt any new behaviour it will feel uncomfortable. This should not be a sign to give up. If anything, if that feeling of discomfort arises when doing something that matters, it is a call to persist.

This captures a quality of committed action that you might call "whole-heartedness". Of course some actions that our coachees take will be small, and we do not insist that every action be profound and life changing. All we do ask though, is that they take these actions consciously and with full commitment, without any qualifiers or "yes buts". This is the difference between the conditional "yes" that they may have been used to giving in the past ("Yes, I will do this thing that matters, as long as the conditions are perfect and I know it will go well") and the unconditional "yes" of ACC ("Yes, I will do this thing that matters, knowing that in doing so uncomfortable experiences will show up, and I cannot guarantee what the outcome will be").

To help coachees to take this step whole-heartedly and with full consciousness you might ask them to consider what type of external and internal obstacles they are likely to face as they pursue a particular action. Once these are clearly expressed, you might ask them to come up with some ways that they can manage these obstacles if and when they show up.

References

Blonna, R. (2011). *Maximize Your Coaching Effectiveness*. Oakland, CA: New Harbinger Publications.

Harris, R. (2009). *ACT Made Simple: An Easy to Read Primer on Acceptance and Commitment Therapy*. Oakland, CA: New Harbinger Publications.

24

Persistence and the power of habit

At its simplest, ACC can be formulated as a combination of mindfulness and values-guided action. We teach our coachees to adopt a mindful perspective towards their thoughts and feelings, not because it is pleasant to be mindful (although it often is!), but because it is a place from which to start taking clear and purposeful action towards their values and goals.

The beauty of this is that it offers coachees a means to take values-guided action moment by moment. However, as humans we only have a limited cognitive capacity – we can only attend consciously to a few things at a time, and the fact remains that we are creatures of habit. The great majority of everything we think, say and do is essentially unconscious and automatic. Through mindfulness we can begin to bring conscious awareness to our experience and notice which of the habits that currently drive our thinking and behaviour are helping us move towards our values and which ones are not. The task then is to use our limited resources of cognitive capacity, time and energy to focus on developing new habits that will move us more purposefully towards our values, and shed those that move us away.

We regard the key skill here as being *flexible persistence*. We stress the "flexible" aspect because we are wary of the idea that persistence in itself is a good thing. *Flexible* persistence is about persisting with a course of action while it is workable, being mindful enough to notice when it is no longer workable, and being willing to change course as required.

"Persistence" often exists alongside the idea of "willpower", and it is the idea of "willpower" as the key ingredient to behaviour change that often proves one of the biggest obstacles to creating new and helpful habits. Buying into the "willpower story" can set our coachees' Thinking Selves to making comparisons ("I'm not as strong-willed as her"), judgements and predictions ("I'm lazy", "I will probably fail, I have no willpower") and seeking answers about something that may be unhelpful anyway ("Why do I have no willpower?")! All that busy work in our minds can mean we end up spending more energy on struggling with the "willpower story" than doing the stuff that might actually be helpful.

The irony is that in trying to control our behaviour, we have to acknowledge a fundamental lack of control over what are usually thought of as the core aspects of "willpower": emotions and thoughts. Part of establishing any new habit will be consciously defusing from the stories that our minds will tell us about "willpower".

A helpful distinction to make when getting started can be between "habits" and "rituals" (Loehr & Schwartz, 2003). Habits are non-conscious behaviours that either may or may not be consistent with our values. Rituals are actions that we take purposefully and consistently, using the limited cognitive capacity available to us and which, through repetition, eventually shift into the unconscious, and become another of the pattern of habits and routines that makes up our daily lives.

In the last chapter we described how to help coachees create workable action plans. The first suggestion was to ensure that they set goals that are consistent with their values. Helping them flexibly persist with these goals, and the rituals which are their building blocks, will be about helping them to stay in touch with those values. This will be particularly important when your coachee experiences disappointment or perceived setbacks. Indeed, an ACC coach can be of great service by helping the coachee to rethink and reframe their perspective on setbacks in general. Our coachees will tend to associate "success" and "failure" on the basis of the outcomes of their actions. Given the ACC focus on values above and beyond goals, we can help coachees to appreciate successes in terms of *the process* of valued living.

For example, Teri has just moved into a team leader role, but has been discussing with her coach that she suspects that her team don't take her seriously. As a result she has been avoiding contact with them, and hasn't held a team meeting in months. In the previous coaching session, Teri identified values of courage and experimentation as ones she would like to work towards by committing to call a team meeting at some point during the next week. When she returns for the next coaching session Teri is dejected.

- Coach: Hey, how did you get on last week in terms of connecting more with your team?
- Teri: Not great … I tried really hard, I was all mindful and even managed to get myself to a place where I was able to call a team meeting but when I did it was like it always has been. They would barely look at or interact with me, I didn't know what to say and ended up babbling to fill the space before just calling it to an end and it felt like a bit of a fail.
- Coach: Sure. And while I get that, I want to make a distinction between the outcomes you'd like to see and the direction that you want to be heading in. It sounds like when you went into that meeting you had in mind that for this to be a success it had to be smooth and the guys had to respond well to you, and you had to be clear and articulate, and if that wasn't the case then it was a failure.
- Teri: Yeah, I guess. That's what I wanted.
- Coach: So, I want to come back to that key thing about values being a direction you head in rather than a destination you reach – qualities that you bring to your actions, ways of being that you aspire to. It sounds to me that even though it wasn't exactly the way you wanted it to be, you still took some important steps in the direction of that value, wouldn't you say?

Keeping focus on the ongoing process of valued living as well as goal achievement is absolutely vital to flexible persistence. Not only does it promote the ongoing development of psychological flexibility and values-led living, it can be harnessed to promote a different and much more adaptive metric for "success". We will discuss this further in Chapter 26 (Working with high performers). By retaining a focus on the values that underpin their goals, our coachees have a much greater chance of developing habits that will propel them towards those goals.

With these principles in mind, there are various practical guidelines we can suggest to coachees to create an environment that will support them in persisting with rituals long enough for them to become habits:

- **Structuring new actions around established routines**: For instance, a coachee who wants to develop a new habit of doing some professional reading every day might choose a specific moment in the day to do so – before bed for example. Or someone who wanted to practise mindfulness each day might choose the car journey home from work as a specific time to do it. These are things that are going to happen anyway. Linking with predictable routines can be a strong anchor for new behaviours.
- **Mindfulness triggers**: None of us can be mindful all of the time, and we never suggest to our coachees that this is a desired outcome. We all have moments of autopilot and that is fine. And, it is useful to have some things that can prompt our coachees to use the mindfulness skills they have learned to come back into the here and now. These might be physical reminders like a wristband which, when they see or feel it, is a prompt to do a mindful check in. Others will use something in their environment – a stone or some other item that might sit on their desk as a reminder. Others use a mindfulness chime on their phone.

- **Tracking progress, rewards and personal high fives**: Most people track their progression towards targets (usually set for them by someone else) at work – why not bring that level of rigour to personal coaching targets? A coachee can use a progress log to give themselves a score out of 10 each day for the degree to which they successfully pursued their goals can work. Rewards along the way for success can be a great supplement, as can encouraging our coachees to give themselves "personal high fives" along the way. For most people what comes naturally is to ruminate on failure and slip-ups. We can encourage our coachees to build a habit around acknowledging and celebrating success.
- **Self-compassion**: As important as celebrating moments of success is allowing for self-compassion in moments where things don't go to plan. There are specific mindfulness exercises focused on accessing the capacity to forgive and value yourself even when things don't go the way you wanted them to.

Reference

Loehr, J., & Schwartz, T. (2003). *The Power of Full Engagement*. New York: Free Press.

25

Mindfulness on the move

When working with coachees – especially in the business world – a very common thought pattern they often fuse with could be referred to as "the busy story". At its simplest, this is the mind saying "I would do x or y that would help me move in the direction of my values, but I can't because I am too busy". This could pose a bit of an obstacle to coaching as even coming to the sessions could be considered yet another thing on the to-do list. Even more so when you consider the mindfulness practice and commitment to taking action that underpins the ACC model.

Now, ideally, if we can help our coachees to focus on what matters and simply notice the stories their minds are telling them, then they will be able to make a clear values-based choice about whether it is a worthwhile investment of their time to practise mindfulness skills! However, it pays to meet people where they are – and to offer them a range of different ways to work the mindfulness muscle, beyond traditional eyes-closed meditative practice.

There are many easy, effective techniques to incorporate mindfulness into the flow of everyday living. And, while their efficiency and ease are a benefit, this is not really about saving time. What we are proposing here is cultivating a mindful approach to the act of living. We can be mindful walking down the street, watching a movie or soothing a crying baby. Once we have a "mindfulness lens" to bring to our experience, every moment is an opportunity for practice.

One of the simplest ways to introduce this is to encourage coachees to mindfully engage in something they would be doing anyway as part of their daily routine, and which they would normally do "on automatic pilot". A mindful shower can be a great place to start – it will probably only last five minutes or so, and is a nice, vivid sensory experience. The advice you would give to the coachee would be to bring the quality of the mindful breathing exercise (Chapter 20, Be here now – helping coachees contact the present moment) to the act of showering.

The general instructions for a mindful shower will be similar to those for mindful breathing. First invite the coachees to consciously pause and switch out of autopilot. Second, to select some part of the sensory experience of showering as an anchor – it could be the feeling of the water on the skin, the sound of the shower-head, the sight of condensation gathering on the wall. Third, fully engage with that sensory experience with openness and curiosity. And, fourth, when they notice their mind wandering into thinking, gently bring it back to the here and now.

As shower is 1) something that most people do everyday, 2) a time when most people are not even *trying* to get anything else done, and 3) something that most people tend to enjoy. Bringing mindful awareness to something enjoyable is a great first on-the-move mindfulness practice. Another great example here is mindful eating or drinking. You can ask your coachee to think of something they eat or drink, which they like, but which they often find themselves consuming mindlessly and on auto-pilot. Typical examples here would be tea and coffee, or biscuits and cookies – things that might be consumed at the desk for a coffee break. Suggest to your coachee that they have a mindful coffee break. There is a small extra level of challenge here as many people will not really be taking a coffee break as such, and will just be eating and drinking while working – there is space here for the "busy story" to get in. But be willing to challenge your coachee to dedicate time – even if just two minutes – to actually taste the coffee they are drinking, the biscuit they are eating, and to engage with it with all of their senses.

These examples are a nice way to embed the idea that mindfulness is not just a tool for being effective, it is a way of engaging more fully with life. However, we need to be careful not to unwittingly promote the idea that mindfulness is to be equated with "pleasant experiences". Mindfulness is, of course, about engaging with whatever is happening here and now, whether it is pleasant or unpleasant, wanted or unwanted. The key is to encourage mindful connection with things that we normally engage with on auto-pilot.

One part of life where many of our coachees report an unhelpful level of auto-pilot is in their relationship with their phones and electronic devices. On that basis we have in the past guided coachees through an exercise about mindfully connecting with a phone (Sinclair & Seydel, 2013). The process is essentially the same as in any other mindfulness exercise. We ask the coachee to hold the device in their hands and then, first, pause; second, consciously connect with a sensory experience (the weight, the feel, the look of the phone); third, to fully engage with that sensory experience (truly noticing the weight, the feel, the appearance with openness and truly naive curiosity); fourth, to notice when the mind has wandered and consciously bring it back.

An extra element we have added in the past has been to then ask the coachee to find a text message or email that they are yet to respond to and – from this place of mindfulness, and with their core values in mind – draft a response. In doing this we make explicit how a mindful perspective and values focus can be used to help us be more effective in our day-to-day lives.

What we are trying to do with all of these examples is to, first circumvent the "busy story", and second encourage our coachees to adopt a mindful approach to life. This implicitly challenges the control agenda by communicating that mindfulness is not a "tool" to be implemented in moments of stress or crisis. These kinds of on-the-move practices can, at best, create a mindfulness habit that will be sustainable, and create a strong foundation for values-based action.

Reference

Sinclair, M., & Seydel, J. (2013). *Mindfulness for Busy People: Turning from Frantic and Frazzled into Calm and Composed.* Harlow, UK: Pearson Education Limited.

26

Working with high performers

The risk when talking about "high performers" (or any arbitrarily assigned group of people) is that we lapse into stereotype and generalisation. What we would wish to offer, however, is that there are some common experiences that might be shared by people who are operating at the top of their field, or who have achieved a high level of success.

One of those experiences may, in fact, be a level of fusion with some self-stories about "success", what it means and what it takes to achieve it. One way in which these stories might show up could be a degree of reluctance or resistance to fully engage with coaching. Someone who has achieved success through one way of approaching their work and life may experience a proposed different way as a threat, or an implicit judgement that they have been doing things is "wrong".

If you do sense that a coachee is presenting with some defensiveness about a "new" way of doing things, a helpful way to frame ACC is as a new set of skills – something to sit alongside and complement the coachee's existing way of operating, rather than to replace it. We can openly acknowledge that whatever they have been doing up until now must be working, because they are sitting here with you, a well-functioning, successful individual. And, we can propose (as we did in Chapter 12, What we talk about when we talk about ACC) that "what got you here won't get you there" – if there is something that the coachee has been striving for and unable to achieve, doing more of the same but harder is unlikely to be helpful. If the coachee wants to take a true leap forward in terms of their development and effectiveness, we can put it to them that a qualitatively different approach could be what is needed.

Often we suggest to our coachee that the world (especially the world of work) is changing rapidly: becoming faster, more interconnected and increasingly volatile. And yet most of us are still using the same skills that we have been relying on for years. You could use the metaphor of trying to run a state of the art smartphone using Windows 95 – we need a new operating system to flourish among the challenges and opportunities of a new world.

Again, this may not always be the case, but it is not uncommon to find that those who are performing at a very high level are doing so at some level of cost to their well-being. Commonly this shows up as a vigorous pursuit of goals having in some way compromised their values. We have worked with many coachees who have achieved great things in their professional lives, but have found that a toll has been taken in terms of their health, self-care, general well-being or personal lives. With such coachees some of our work might be about reframing what is meant by "success".

As coaches, we must remain clear that our aim is to help our coachees in developing a psychologically flexible outlook, with a focus on values above and beyond goals. In Chapter 23 (Helping coachees take committed action) we emphasised the importance of guiding coachees in creating values-consistent objectives, and on prioritising valued living over relentless pursuit of goals. While this may feel counterintuitive to our more goal-orientated coachees, there is a way of framing this that many find to be extremely empowering.

Fred Kofman (2006) talks about "success beyond success". According to Kofman, success as measured by external outcomes (sales, promotion, remuneration) can only ever be partially within any individual's control. To at least some degree the attainment of these outcomes will be dependent on other factors – environmental factors, economic factors, other people, plain luck. So to gauge how "successful" one is on this basis is necessarily to outsource a large and important part of one's self-image. However, success as measured by the degree to which one is true to and consistent in acting on one's values as we strive towards our goals is entirely within our control. This is what Kofman refers to as "success beyond success".

In our experience, this is often received by even the most high-achieving, goal-oriented coachees as an extremely attractive new way of framing their idea of what it is to be "successful". Not only does it place an emphasis on their own authorship and autonomy, it helps them to truly connect with deeper values that they might not have consciously considered previously. Indeed, often it is those who have been operating at a high level, perhaps at the expense of their values, who engage with these conversations about success through values most enthusiastically.

With such coachees we would still talk explicitly about goals and actions, and we would also direct them very specifically to focus more consciously and specifically on their values. In Chapter 24 (Persistence and the power of habit), we recommended asking coachees to keep a progress log of their success in taking action towards their goals each day. Here we would suggest asking coachees to keep a similar log tracking the degree to which they were true to their core values each day.

With this reorientation towards values, we are hopefully helping our coachee to connect with a type of "success" that is more within their control, which is at a deeper level of personal connection, and which is – crucially – also more sustainable. A focus on goals over, or at the expense of, values will come at a personal cost in the long run. The metaphor that is pertinent here is that of life being a "marathon rather than a sprint". Sustainable success is not achievable without a focus on values. It is those who lose this perspective who tend to fall victim to chronic stress or burnout.

There are likely to be a number of powerful self-stories underlying the kind of driven behaviour that disconnects coachees from their values and puts them at risk of burnout. During a workshop we were delivering once with a group of senior leaders in a technology company, one group member asked the others "Who thinks they are lazy?". One by one, the vast majority of the hands in the room went up. Only moments earlier we had been talking about how most of them were working incredibly long hours and were struggling to maintain their life balance. And, it seemed, many of them were being driven to do so by the "I'm lazy" story.

Helping our coachees to get eyes on these stories, and to make a conscious decision about whether they are helpful in the moment will be crucial. Here some of the exercises around strengthening connection with the Observing Self mentioned in Chapter 21 (Introducing self as context) might be helpful.

When we use a term like "high performers" one's mind may turn to the world of sport. Often athletes will talk about being "in the zone" or "in flow" – a space where they are operating at peak performance in a way that feels effortless and almost unconscious. While people in the world of work may use different terminology, they will often find themselves in that same space. And while we would not wish to disrupt this when it is working well, the question might be how to remain open, aware and active when at the limits of performance. Here what might be useful could be some of the techniques mentioned in Chapter 24 (Persistence and the power of habit), such as mindfulness chimes, physical anchors to encourage the coachee to pause momentarily for a mindful check-in. In these short moments they can simply notice what is going on inside and around them – any thoughts from which they may need to defuse, any feelings for which they may need to make space – check in with their values and make a conscious choice as to their next action.

Reference

Kofman, F. (2006). *Conscious Business: How to Build Value Through Values*. Boulder, CO: Sounds True.

27

Managing tricky or unexpected moments

A question we hear over and over again when we train or supervise coaches is a version of "What if it all goes horribly, terribly wrong?!". This is an excellent question and we appreciate that sometimes this query stems from the natural and normal concerns about stepping out of a cosy, comfort zone and into the great unknown. Here it's helpful to check in with the ACC processes for yourself. Can you drop into the present moment, notice the thoughts and feelings as they ebb and flow and with curiosity, bring your values compass out and use that as a guide to your next move?

We also appreciate sometimes "curveballs" or unexpected moves from coachees occur and it's useful to prepare and plan a little for these kinds of situations. So, here we've compiled the top three questions we get asked in training and supervision related to curveballs.

1. *My coachee has been sent to see me by their manager/ occupational health/their partner and they clearly don't want to be there. What do I do?*

Having a coachee being coerced into coaching is tricky and needs to be addressed from the outset. In the majority of situations it's possible to disengage from the coaching relationship if a coachee really doesn't want to be there. If that is the case, and they are adamant they are not interested, then the most helpful course of action is of course to wrap up the session.

Having said that, if there is some wiggle room and the coachee isn't immediately dashing to the door, there are four steps that are likely to be helpful to increase the chances that they may choose to stay (or least be in a position to make their choice based on values).

First, normalise and validate the coachee's position. This has the effect of reducing antagonism towards you and increasing the chances of teamwork happening. This could be a statement like:

> *It's completely understandable you're feeling reluctant to be here. Anyone in your situation would probably feel exactly the same.*

Second, declare your intention to be helpful to the coachee in meeting their goals (and not the goals of whoever sent them to coaching), even if this means ending the session and not proceeding.

Third, be straightforward and open in clarifying any practical consequences of not proceeding, without being punitive. This may include for example, discussing any summary reports you're required to produce.

Last, remind the coachee that they are able to choose if they want to proceed, but perhaps the choice could be made consciously, based on what's personally important to them, rather than on the basis of the particular feelings that are present at that moment. It's often worth suggesting using the session to help the coachee do this.

2. *My coachee can't identify any feelings!*

As an approach, ACC does tend to ask a lot about our coachee's emotional landscape compared to contexts that emphasise productivity, efficiency and meeting of results. As such, some coachees may not be used to this emphasis and can initially struggle. However, it's worth first considering some of the possibilities for why clients can find it difficult to talk about emotions. In our experience, there are two main reasons coaching coachees struggle to identify emotions:

First, they worry about consequences of disclosing. Here the coach needs to understand what consequences the coachee is concerned about. For example, being judged, criticised or misunderstood. It's important to normalise and validate these concerns, while at the same time connecting up the purpose to talking about emotions with the client's goals and values. It's useful to allow time for rapport to develop and the coachee to build up a model of the coach as someone who listens carefully and is non-judgemental.

Second, they don't have the vocabulary. In this case, the coach needs to work to help the coachee build up a lexicon related to emotions and assist the client with connecting situations, thoughts, behaviours and physical sensations. In this way, over time, the coachee learns to make these connections by using the various cues to label emotions.

3. *My coachee can be defensive and obstructive*

This can include a full range of behavioural patterns, such as being argumentative, shutting down and not talking, or doing lots of "yes, buts ..." (i.e. *yes*, making that change is a great idea, *but* here are 501 reasons why I couldn't possibly do it).

Assuming the coachee does actually want to be in coaching sessions (if not, see point 1 above), then the following three handy steps usually help:

First, name it. Pause the session and bring it out of automatic pilot mode. Gently spotlight the behaviour in a way to engender some curiosity in the coachee.

> *I just want to draw your attention to something interesting I see happening in the session. I see you ... [objectively describe the behaviour].*

Second, normalise it. Following on from above, normalise the behaviour to reduce the sense that you are being critical or judgemental.

> *Of course, there's nothing wrong with it and it's totally normal – and I understand why you might do it.*

Third, notice the impact on values and goals. Bring the session goals and values into the picture as a way to evaluate the behaviour – not as good or bad, but as helpful or less helpful in moving towards values. Then suggest using skills learned so far as an opportunity to directly work with what's showing up in the session.

> *I might be wrong here, but I notice that when it's happening, the goals and values we've been focusing on seem that little bit further away. If that were that case, would you be willing to try out some of the skills we've been working on right here and now?*

28

Six mistakes we have made (and what we learned)

Making mistakes can be one of our greatest educators in developing a good coaching practice. But it's not just about making mistakes. Repeating mistakes over and over tends not to be much fun. It's about leaning into the mistakes, even when they come with a twinge of embarrassment or hit our failure button. Leaning in so we can figure out how to do it differently next time. At the same time, it is also useful to learn off other people's mistakes; so to give you full advantage of our many failures, we're going to offer up our top six mistakes in the hope that you can learn from us.

Metaphor overload

ACT is packed full of useful metaphors that are fun and creative. There's opportunities to play with them (the polygraph metaphor), act them out (tug-of-war with the monster), create visual metaphors (e.g. on the dance floor) or watch animations (for example *The Unwelcome Party Guest*, www.youtube.com/watch? v=VYht-guymF4).

Coachees will often respond well to the introduction of a metaphor. Metaphors tend to be fun and creative, and if they're working well, illuminate new perspectives in helpful ways. As such we've often fallen into the trap of hurling multiple metaphors at a coachee in a session, ending up overloading and confusing them.

Our recommendation is to carefully choose a metaphor, think about the purpose of it and where possible, link to the coachee's own sphere of experience (see Chapter 17, Use of metaphor). As a general rule, anything more than one metaphor a session runs the risk of confusing the coachee. Best is where a central metaphor can be introduced and then developed over a number of sessions.

Failure to clarify goals

You're three sessions into a coaching piece and starting to feel a little at sea. When you sit down to plan your next session, you ask yourself, "What are we supposed to be working on?" and you realise you haven't nailed down tight, focused goals with your coachee.

We've both made the mistake many times of not fixing these early on and then paying the price at a later stage. *Everyone* in coaching knows this is important but it can be so easy to let slip. Goals give your session purpose, direction and structure. Of course, obstacles to these values-based goals will arise, but that then becomes grist for the mill in your coaching sessions together.

Buying the coachee's story

Talking about values and helping coachees take steps in valued directions is perhaps one of the most rewarding parts of ACC work. And inevitably, it brings coachees right up against all the reasons, rules and stories for why change is just not possible. And it can be easy to slip into equally buying the coachee's story as true. In an ACC group training session, we worked with a coachee who wanted to build resilience skills to manage the impact of a very busy role as lead editor in a successful publishing company. The story they brought to the group went something like:

I love the pressure of my job; it's exciting and thrilling, even if it's sometimes very stressful. And if I slow down my pace, there are 10 other junior editors who will pounce to take my place. I'll lose my job, won't be able to pay my mortgage and I'll end up in the gutter!

We both noticed our minds agreeing with the coachee, not seeing any place to move. This lead to lots of acknowledgement of the difficult position but not much change!

Key for the coach is to notice this process and the narrowing effect it has. And help the coachee to recognise this process. Absolutely, there was a truth to this thought. And, buying it wholesale hugely reduced the possibility of flexible mindful responding and the chances of a creative solution arising.

From an ACC perspective, these same processes of fusion apply to coaches as well. But the good news is that equally, we coaches can also use the same skills to unhook. Thank you for that thought, mind ...

Instruction rather than experience

There's absolutely nothing wrong with some judicious instruction. That being said, ACC is an experiential model. This means that underpinning behavioural learning principles suggest that developing new ways of responding to thoughts and feelings are most likely to occur through actually experiencing them, rather than being told about them. This is the difference between being told how to skydive versus actually doing it. There's no comparison. It's important for the coach to set a context within which the coachee can try out skills live. This could mean practising present moment exercises, noticing and defusing from thoughts live as they are occurring or setting up opportunities for values-based actions live in session.

Not taking risks and doing novel things

Linked to the above point, an ACC intervention can ask a lot of a coach. Being active, trying out exercises and doing new things can feel risky – it's stepping out of a comfort zone. It's far easier to stick to talking about things, being guided by the coachee and not doing things that may seem, at face value, a bit whacky – or might be judged by our coachees as whacky. But in the space of newness and difference, is the place where, with a well-designed exercise, coachees can learn new skills, develop new perspectives and move forward. The onus is then on us to catch our own stories, hold these lightly and act in the service of our own values.

Not calling out interfering behaviours

Except for the ever so slightly sadistic among us, most coaches don't find it that easy to spotlight unhelpful or interfering behaviours in our coachees. Such behaviours can include talking too much to avoid difficult subjects, defensive or prickly reactions to feedback, trying to catch a coach out ("How old are you?", "What are your qualifications?", "Do you really think you can help someone as successful as me?"). But not doing so eats into valuable time, and often deprives a coachee of invaluable, honest feedback on their own behaviour. Like a physical workout, a good coaching session is probably going to be more helpful if it's more about pushing up against limits and stretching a bit than a gentle massage and a nice sauna. Of course there is nothing wrong with this, but if change is in order, it's often going to take a bit more than that.

Having an agreement with your coachee where they allow you to give feedback, both on behaviours that work and those that don't, is a great way to set up the expectation for this and get their consent.

| 29

A simple six-session ACC model

Good ACC should be undertaken and applied with lots of flexibility in order to be most responsive to the coachee's needs. As such, it's difficult to be prescriptive about exactly what should be included in a coaching protocol. Keeping this in mind, this chapter sets out a six-session modular structure for ACC that we use within our coaching work.

Session 1: Assessment, formulation and values-based goal setting

Key aims

- Active assessment
- Introduce the Matrix
- Introduce mindfulness

The first session focuses on carrying out an "active assessment" in which the three key components of relationship building, direction setting and information gathering are developed (see Chapter 13, Assessment).

Towards the end of this first session, the coach summarises everything discussed so far using the Matrix (see Chapter 14, The Matrix) to draw this together. You can use a Matrix form or simply draw it out on a piece of paper or whiteboard. There are several components to this, the first of which is to outline values and values-based actions as the coachee has described them. Along with this, the coachee is helped to notice "away moves" in order to discriminate between internal content (thoughts, emotions) and behaviour that functions to move away from this content. It's important to link the ways in which such actions can interfere with values-based actions and the goals the coachee has articulated, while at the same time normalising these experiences. This begins to develop the message that it's not the thoughts and feelings that are necessarily problematic, just that the responses to them interfere with towards moves.

At this point, mindfulness can be introduced as an alternative skill to automatic responding and as an aid to values-based responding. Out-of-session work is suggested to consolidate ideas and prepare for Session 2.

Out-of-session work

Over the week, use the Matrix review to notice one towards move and one away move each day until the next session to build mindful noticing skills.

Session 2: Offering a new, mindfully aware perspective – the Matrix

Key aims

- Review homework
- Revisit matrix
- Values clarification
- Build mindfulness skills

Review

Review the out-of-session work set at the end of Session 1. As it's common for coachees not to complete the homework, this time can be used to retrospectively recall towards and away moves over the week. Use this to also review the concept of the Matrix by using what the coachee noticed and filling in a Matrix diagram.

Values clarification

Introduce the compass metaphor (see Chapter 10, Values) and use this to move into a card-sort values clarification exercise (see Chapter 22, What really matters). Use the values generated from this exercise and link it to the goals the coachee described in Session 1.

Mindful pauses

A mindful breathing space is introduced as a method to practically step out of auto-pilot, develop a present moment awareness and notice thoughts and feelings. The coach practises this in the session with the coachee and invites reflection and feedback (see Chapter 20, Be here now). It is useful to link this practice to the task of undertaking values-based actions and propose it as a method to begin to unhook from unwanted thoughts and feelings.

Out-of-session work

Invite the coachee to think of a small values-based action they would be willing to take over the week. Frame it as a "noticing exercise", where the coachee has the opportunity to step out of auto-pilot in order to mindfully notice their experience. Ask the coachee what experiences may hook them and prevent them from undertaking the values-based action.

Suggest to the coachee that they practise the mindful breathing exercise completed within the session. It can be helpful to record the actual exercise carried out in session and give this to the coachee. Mobile phone recorders make this very easy. Ask the coachee to make notes of what they experienced during this practice.

Session 3: Practising mindful aware skills and unhooking from thoughts

Key aims

- Further present moment practice
- Practise unhooking from thoughts

Review

Review the scheduled out-of-session work with the coachee, asking about what they observed in relation to both the values-based action task and the mindfulness exercise. If the coachee wasn't able to complete the tasks, ask with curiosity about any hooks that showed up. Also ask about other values-based actions that occurred.

- Mindful check in
- Carry out mindful breathing exercise

Unhooking from thoughts

In this session, focus on skills for unhooking from unhelpful thoughts. It particularly helps to use thoughts the coachee has described over the past sessions that they have experienced as unwanted or unhelpful. Introduce the Flaxman manoeuvre (Chapter 15, Formulation) as a metaphor to structure the point of unhooking from thoughts in the context of values. This reinforces the notion that the task is not to eliminate thoughts, but to de-emphasise their importance and make values a more prominent guide to behaviour. From here, practise methods to unhook from thoughts in-session, including the "I'm noticing I'm having the thought that ..." exercise and "leaves on the stream" exercise (Chapter 18, Facilitating cognitive defusion).

Out-of-session work

- Practise mindful breathing exercise
- Practise unhooking from thoughts
- Set further values-based actions

Session 4: Working skilfully with emotion and developing resilience

Key aims

- Develop skills to work effectively with emotion

Review

Debrief on the out-of-session work and make time to check in with the coachee about progress and trouble shoot any issues that have arisen.

All the previous sessions have worked to develop the message to emphasise building an accepting stance towards internal experiences. In this session, introduce exercises to explicitly practise an accepting and non-judgemental stance. Practise the "physicalising exercise (Chapter 19, From struggle to acceptance).

Link this exercise in with the previous sessions, and how a defused, open stance towards emotion requires mindful awareness. Also link in the ways that this stance can be used to facilitate values-based actions.

Out-of-session work

- Further mindfulness practice
- Set further values-based actions

Session 5: Revisiting values and focusing on "success beyond success" performance

Key aims

- Revisit values

Review

Debrief on the out-of-session work and make time to check in with the coachee about progress and trouble shoot any issues that have arisen.

Values revisit

Come back to the values that the coachee described in the first and second sessions. Use the values compass diagram to measure progress towards value actions and goals. Specifically ask about what the coachee has learned over the sessions in terms of what is important to them and what it is like to engage in these values. Also ask about learning in relation to hooks and auto-pilot responses. Ask about any feedback from external sources on their work they have undertaken (family, friends, managers etc.).

Out-of-session work

- Further mindfulness practice
- Set further values-based actions

Session 6: Review and planning for the future

Review progress made in terms of actions taken and also skills building achievements. This is an opportunity to congratulate the coachee on their progress and make clear explicit links between their progress and skills development. It's also useful to reflect on work still to be done. This can be used to develop an action plan for going forward in the future.

It's helpful to discuss any potential pitfalls in the future that might arise and a plan for managing these based on skills developed so far. These can be built in to the action plan for the future.

ACC for group coaching, training and development

So far the context of all the examples we have given has been one-to-one coaching. However, ACC can easily be applied in group settings. Most of the research data around ACT in non-clinical working populations referenced in Chapter 4 (ACT coaching research) is based on group work. These studies were interventions for workplace well-being and mental health. This is the primary context in which work-based ACC coaching and training takes place, and it is a proven effective way of developing individual and team well-being and resilience.

There is reason to believe that ACC in groups may actually be the optimum way of working. There are a number of advantages of group work over one-to-one interventions – specific ways in which the core ACC processes can be demonstrated, experimented with and enhanced, which are less accessible in one-to-one coaching.

One of these advantages is around use of metaphor. In Chapter 17 (Use of metaphor) we described the process by which ACC metaphors evoke behavioural change. All of the examples we used to illustrate this were verbal metaphors. However, there are also more active, physical metaphors that, while they can be used in a one-to-one context, come to life more vividly when acted out in a group setting.

One classic example would be the "passengers on the bus" metaphor. The central metaphorical concept of "passengers on the bus" is that living life is like driving a bus. As we travel in the direction of our values we carry with us a number of passengers (thoughts, feelings, memories, sensations) who can distract us from the road if we attend to or struggle with them too much. However, if we can just notice them and use mindfulness skills to defuse from and accept the presence of those "passengers", then we can continue to focus on the road ahead and move in the direction of our values. In a group setting, this can be acted out dramatically, to bring the various components alive in a memorable way. The facilitator can guide a participant through a situation that they are struggling with, while other group members physically represent the valued direction, and the various unhelpful passenger voices. By physically enacting the movement towards values, the struggle with internal content (literally voiced by other group members) and experimenting with different ways of responding (struggling, giving in and willingness), the metaphor becomes more vivid and the impact more memorable. A video example of "passengers on the bus" being acted out and instructions for delivery in a group are available at https://contextualconsulting.co.uk/insights/passengers-on-the-bus-metaphor-acting-out-in-a-group.

Of course, in the above example the individual who represents the "driver" of the bus benefits from actively working through a challenging situation in the group. However, the other participants inevitably benefit too. "Passengers on the bus" is a metaphor that can be applied to almost any situation. This reflects another potential benefit of group interventions – the opportunity for participants to learn from each other and share experiences.

In particular, the group setting represents an opportunity for participants to experiment with different ways of responding to unwanted internal experiences. The facilitator can create an environment and structure experiences that encourage participants to practise willingness and acceptance. One exercise designed for a group setting, and that aims to do this, is often simply known as the "labels exercise". Group participants are asked to bring to mind a word or phrase about themselves that their mind often gets hooked by, usually one that has a strong element of self-judgement, and to then write this down on a label. They are then invited to stick that label to their chest and walk around the room in silence looking at other people's labels, while willingly allowing others to look at their own. In doing so it is very likely that many challenging private experiences will show up. In debriefing their experience of the exercise at the end, participants can experiment with opening up to and even publicly acknowledging these experiences, while also having them normalised by others sharing their own. This creates an opportunity to model defusion and acceptance in the context of a valued action (connecting in a meaningful way with others).

While a coach can model openness and acceptance in one-to-one sessions, doing so in a group setting is perhaps even more influential. Being willing to publicly own your own humanity, fallibility and moments of struggle with the group is very powerful. This can be done at any time during a session, but a good moment to set the stage for this is when explaining your role at the beginning of a group. Very helpful here is the "two mountains" metaphor. This is a neat way of establishing the nature of the ACC coaching relationship – one of common humanity and essential equality between coach and coachee. Here the coach asks the coachees to imagine that they are all like mountaineers. The coachees are "over there" climbing their mountains, trying their best, sometimes making great progress, sometimes stumbling or getting lost. And the coach is "over here", also on her mountain, progressing and struggling in kind. The coach doesn't have all the answers and has by no means scaled her mountain. However, what she does have from over on her mountain is a perspective that the coachees – with their noses to the cliff-face of their own mountains – do not have. She can use this to point out potential hand-holds or approaching obstacles that they might not have seen.

As well as personally modeling willingness and acceptance, the coach can encourage group members to do the same. With the right atmosphere of confidentiality, non-judgement and respect, people will be willing to talk about their successes and struggles. In doing so it becomes clear to the other group members that we all have unwanted thoughts and feelings, that we all get stuck from time to time. In doing so, the group also helps to highlight the key ACC principle that it is not the unwanted experiences (which we all have) that tend to be the problem, but the struggle against them.

As this stuff is discussed in the group, the participants will inevitably get opportunities to notice themselves and others in moments of internal struggle and avoidance, and also to witness themselves and others modeling acceptance and willingness and acting on their values. Again, the learning that comes from witnessing others doing this (and being witnessed by others) is in advance of what might be possible in a normal one-to-one coaching session. By its nature, ACC is active and experiential, and the group setting offers particular scope for this kind of learning.

In terms of values and committed action, a great benefit of a group context is the opportunity for idea sharing and a consistent accountability system. When entire teams work together they can commit to common practices that support psychological flexibility. One example would be a morning "check in" where team members can share anything they want that feels important, personal or professional, successes or struggles. In Organisation and Relationship Systems Coaching (ORSC) there is a practice called the Designed Team Alliance (DTA). It is an open conversation among colleagues about their shared culture, where they discuss the values they want to work towards and the behaviours they want to promote as a team. Even if the group you are working with are not direct colleagues, there is still a great opportunity for participants to offer advice and input to one another, and to hold one another accountable for actions they have committed to taking.

There is no one prescribed format for ACC group interventions – the model is flexible enough to allow for multiple short sessions (perhaps over the course of a lunch hour), or one or more full-day sessions. However, one of the most well-used protocols takes the form of a "two plus one" model, with the first two sessions delivered in consecutive weeks, and the third following after a month or so. Flaxman, Bond, and Livheim (2013) describe this protocol and give invaluable input around how to tailor individual and group interventions in their book *The Mindful and Effective Employee.*

Reference

Flaxman, P., Bond, F., & Livheim, F. (2013). *The Mindful and Effective Employee: An Acceptance and Commitment Therapy Training Manual for Improving Well-being and Performance.* Oakland, CA: New Harbinger Publications.

Index

Page numbers in *italics* refer to figures.

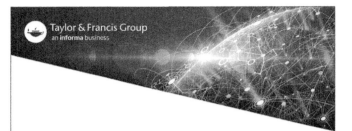

Printed in Great Britain
by Amazon

19797604R00088